History of Southeast Asia

A Captivating Guide to the History of a Vast Region Containing Countries Such as Cambodia, Laos, Thailand, Singapore, Indonesia, Burma, and More

Free Bonus from Captivating History
(Available for a Limited time)

Hi History Lovers!

Now you have a chance to join our exclusive history list so you can get your first history ebook for free as well as discounts and a potential to get more history books for free! Simply visit the link below to join.

Captivatinghistory.com/ebook

Also, make sure to follow us on Facebook, Twitter and Youtube by searching for Captivating History.

Contents

INTRODUCTION 1

CHAPTER 1 – THE FIRST FRUITS OF BURMA 3

CHAPTER 2 – CAMBODIA COMES ONTO THE SCENE 9

CHAPTER 3 – THE RISE OF THE KINGDOM OF VIETNAM 18

CHAPTER 4 –THAILAND AND ITS EARLY KINGDOMS 24

CHAPTER 5: THE POLITICAL INTRIGUE OF ANCIENT
INDONESIA 30

CHAPTER 6 – BURMA AND THE BRITISH 38

CHAPTER 7 – VIETNAM, LAOS, AND CAMBODIA OPENED TO
THE WORLD 46

CHAPTER 8– ISLANDS OF DISCOVERY—THE PHILIPPINES 51

CHAPTER 9 – THE COMING OF THE COLONISTS AND
CAPITALISTS 55

CHAPTER 10 – SOUTHEAST ASIA CONSUMED BY THE CO-
PROSPERITY SPHERE 65

CHAPTER 11 – SOUTHEAST ASIA AND THE SWEET TASTE OF
FREEDOM 79

CONCLUSION: WHERE LEGEND MEETS REALITY 92

HERE'S ANOTHER BOOK BY CAPTIVATING HISTORY THAT YOU
MIGHT LIKE 94

FREE BONUS FROM CAPTIVATING HISTORY (AVAILABLE FOR A
LIMITED TIME) 95

APPENDIX A: FURTHER READING AND REFERENCE 96

Introduction

It can be said that there was a human presence in Southeast Asia at least as far back as 40,000 years ago. For it was around this time, during the last Ice Age, that archaeologists have traced prehistoric human settlements in places such as Borneo, Flores, and Java. It is believed that during the last Ice Age, when sea levels were much lower, these islands were actually a part of the mainland. This meant that early human travelers from Asia could have easily walked across land bridges to settle the regions. However, the climate change caused by the melting of glaciers some 10,000 years ago rendered these early human inhabitants islanders rather than simply the dwellers of a continental coastline. There is no written record of these early Southeast Asians, but the trappings of civilization that they left behind are still being dug up by teams of archaeologists to this very day.

In fact, in 2004, a major discovery was made when an early human ancestor, said to have been 18,000 years old, was unearthed. These skeletal remains were similar to modern humans except for the fact that their maximum height appeared to be just three and a half feet. This led some to dub these ancient Southeast Asians as hobbits—as in J. R. R. Tolkien's fantastical tale of the same name. Researchers are still not sure whether these mysterious islanders were simply a shorter version of early *Homo sapiens* (modern humans) or were perhaps closer related to an earlier human predecessor such as *Homo erectus*—an upright walking primate with some human attributes.

After the last Ice Age came to a close, the residents of Southeast Asia quickly learned to adapt to their environment. The powerful rivers that cut their course through the lands of Southeast Asia provided for a rise in rich agriculture. It has been suggested that it was in the fertile valleys of Vietnam, Thailand, and Burma that some of the first agricultural settlements arose, with some dating back to around 8000 BCE. In places such as Thailand, Vietnam, Java, Bali, and the Philippines, the people learned methods so they could take advantage of the wet environment, allowing them to produce well-irrigated rice farms. The self-sustaining nature of these farms would fuel the great Southeast Asian civilizations yet to come. The wet environment also encouraged the use of boats for transportation from one place to another. As scattered as the regions of Southeast Asia are, this transport ensured a continuing cross-cultural dialogue between the various peoples of this area.

Southeast Asians had to learn to adapt to their environment, and their ingenuity is seen in the very nature of their settlements. Since the region is prone to flooding, a different style of housing had to be developed. This included a raised platform, meaning it was above ground. By having this, the water could flow under the structure and not flood into the home. These structures, known as stilt houses, still dominate the Southeast Asian landscape today.

Chapter 1 – The First Fruits of Burma

"You most likely know it as Myanmar, but it will always be Burma to me."

-John O' Hurley

Although today we know it by another name, the nation now known as Myanmar has long been called Burma. The country is situated on the mainland, southwest of China, and its first known residents are said to have lived in the region sometime around 11,000 BCE. Archaeological evidence of these early Burmese settlers has been found scattered along the Irrawaddy River, which flows through lower and upper Burma.

Around 1500 BCE, these settlers were using bronze tools and engaging in widespread agriculture. Burma entered into the Iron Age around 500 BCE, and by the 2nd century BCE, natives who spoke a Tibeto-Burman dialect stepped into the realm of recorded history. The Tibeto-Burmans lived in a network of settlements that date back to 200 BCE, and it was from these that the first city-states would form.

Due to Burma's prime location between India and China, these city-states would become heavily involved with trade between two of the major powers of Asia. This trade of goods also brought a trade of culture and ideas, with one of the most transformative being the religion of Buddhism. The Buddhist faith began in India, but it never really caught on with the people of its native soil. Today, India is predominantly Hindu with sizable percentages of both Muslims and Christians, but very few are Buddhists.

Just as Christianity began in Israel and was exported to surrounding lands, so, too, was Buddhism launched from its point of origin to take root in other nations. Buddhism, at least as it pertains to Burma, dates back to at least the 3rd century BCE. These ties of culture and religion maintained a loose confederation among the old city-states of Burma, but Burma would not become a true nation until the rise of the Pagan dynasty in 849 CE.

The Pagan dynasty, also sometimes called the "Bagan" dynasty, is not to be confused with the religious practice of paganism. The Pagan dynasty is derived from a Burmese city named Pagan, in which the Pagan dynasty was centered. The Pagan Kingdom was primarily in control of northern Burma.

Meanwhile, in the south, another kingdom, known as the Mon Kingdom, began to expand. The two kingdoms existed in a state of rivalry until the Pagan Kingdom managed to defeat the Mon Kingdom in 1057 CE, overrunning the former Mon capital of Thaton in the process. This was a devastating loss for the Mon Kingdom, and it's said that the Pagan Kingdom took some 30,000 prisoners in the aftermath.

Among these captives were quite a few Theravada Buddhists. Over time, these Buddhists began to successfully convert their captors to their faith. Although Buddhism, in general, had been known to the Pagans before, it was the Mon captives who proved to be the most successful missionaries. The Mon alphabet also replaced the Pagan traditional

Sanskrit script, and terminology derived from the Mon people is still prevalent in Burma to this very day.

After the Pagan Kingdom's defeat of the Mon Kingdom, the realm's reach was consolidated under the powerful King Anawrahta. The details on Anawrahta's rule are scarce, but his legacy was undoubtedly great all the same. In fact, it was great enough to survive his death in 1077, the year his much less competent son, Sawlu, took over.

It's said that Sawlu proved to be so inept that a major rebellion of the Mons erupted in the southern portion of the kingdom in 1084. Sawlu died in the conflict, but his half-brother, Kyanzittha, was able to quickly right the ship, and with the reliable apparatus of the state and military in his hands, he quickly put down the unrest and returned the realm to stability. After getting the kingdom back in order, Kyanzittha proved himself to be a great reformer. Under his leadership, the Pagan Kingdom took measures to standardize laws and customs in the region. This was done with the intention of preventing future rebellions, such as the one that had rocked the kingdom at the beginning of Kyanzittha's reign.

Kyanzittha also made efforts to reach out to the nearby powerhouse of China. By the 12th century, the Pagan Kingdom was powerful enough that it had been duly acknowledged by China's Song dynasty and India's Chola dynasty. However, the Pagans would meet their end when they were invaded by the Mongol hordes led by Kublai Khan.

The ever-encroaching Mongols finally defeated China's Song dynasty in 1279. They then swept down from their holdings in China and began to conduct raids in Southeast Asia, leading to the sacking of the capital city of Pagan in 1287. The leadership of the Pagan Kingdom managed to escape the Mongol grasp, and after they fled, they set up shop farther afield. The Mongols eventually left, but what remained of the Pagan Kingdom was fractured and divided into several self-governing parts.

At the dawn of the 1300s, the main polities of Burma consisted of the regional powers of Lower Burma, Upper Burma, Arakan, and the so-called Shan States. The term "Shan" is actually a name designated for the people of Burma who traditionally speak Tai. And as one might imagine, the Shan States are geographically close to modern-day Thailand, as well as bordering China and Laos. These regional conglomerates were then further divided into various principalities and districts.

As one might imagine, these fractured states were often in discord with each other, and this period would come to have an endless series of conflicts and political intrigue. It wasn't until 1364 that a major player once again came to the Burmese stage in the form of the Kingdom of Ava. Centered around the city of Ava near the Irrawaddy and Myitnge Rivers in Upper Burma, the Kingdom of Ava sought to consolidate not just political power in the region but also cultural power.

The Kingdom of Ava supported the Burmese traditions and became associated as the true inheritor kingdom of the Pagan dynasty. One of the more able rulers of the Kingdom of Ava was a man named Mingyi Swasawke, who ruled from 1367 to 1400. During King Swasawke's reign, a more centralized governing structure was created in Upper Burma.

Unfortunately, the Kingdom of Ava would be the subject of multiple conflicts over the next two centuries and would ultimately be threatened by the neighboring Toungoo Kingdom, which was located in Lower Burma. The so-called Toungoo dynasty dates back to King Mingyi Nyo, who established his court in 1510. King Mingyi Nyo's son, Tabinshwehti, would successfully reunite the remnants of the old Pagan Kingdom.

King Tabinshwehti was a competent and able ruler, and he passed on a vibrant and dynamic kingdom to the man who would succeed him: his trusted general, Bayinnaung Kyawhtin Nawrahta. Bayinnaung would deal the deathblow to the Kingdom of Ava by conquering Ava itself in

1555. The Toungoo dynasty would ultimately control much of the former Pagan Kingdom, but after Bayinnaung passed away in 1581, the principalities he had governed became difficult for his subsequent successors to hang onto.

Things came to a head in 1599 when Arakan, with the help of some soldiers of fortune from Portugal, stormed the major trade city of Pegu (modern-day Bago) and eventually instigated the entire collapse of the Toungoo Kingdom. However, the Arakan were betrayed by their Portuguese allies, and they were shocked to see them break rank and create their own small puppet kingdom in Lower Burma.

Portuguese mercenary Filipe de Brito must have had some delusions of grandeur when he tried to set up his own principality based out of the port city and trading hub of Thanlyin in the year 1603. The Toungoo dynasty was not going to take this lying down, however, and just a few years later, the Toungoo king had rallied his forces under the leadership of Nyaungyan Min, who consolidated Upper Burma by 1606.

However, it was actually the one who succeeded him— Anaukpetlun—who managed to drive the Portuguese from Thanlyin, doing so in the year 1613. The restored Toungoo dynasty would then continue to reign over Burma until 1752 when they were toppled by the Hanthawaddy troops of the Mon people. The city of Ava was burned to the ground, the king was deposed, and the rest of the royal family were put in chains.

After their stunning victory, the Mon people rolled right in and established the so-called Restored Hanthawaddy Kingdom. This incarnation of Burmese political power would be brief, as it was superseded by the Konbaung dynasty, which, by 1759, had managed to piece together all of the former polities of Burma. The Konbaung dynasty faced pressure from Chinese forces in the east, and from 1765 to 1769, it would be subjected to four different assaults on Burmese territory, which were all waged by the Qing dynasty.

Penned in by the Chinese in the northeast, the Burmese forces began to expand their territory to the west instead. While this allowed for expansion without provoking the Chinese, it led to the Konbuang's Burmese border to come in close proximity of what was then British-controlled territory in India. The subsequent wars with Britain would eventually lead to a long and costly colonization process.

Chapter 2 – Cambodia Comes onto the Scene

"Let me reassure that the Kingdom of Cambodia, a country with independence, neutrality, peace, freedom, democracy and human rights as you all have seen, shall be existing with no end."

-Hun Sen

It's thanks to ancient Chinese records that we have historical documentation of the very first major governing body to come to prominence in Cambodia. This governing civilization was the Kingdom of Funan, which took root in the 1ˢᵗ century CE. The name "Funan" is of Chinese origin, and it is unlikely that the actual inhabitants of the region called their government by this name. It has been theorized that the Chinese called the kingdom Funan as a geographical designation since it seems to be the Chinese version of the Khmer (a language of Cambodia) word *vnam*, which means mountain. Whatever the case may be, and for the lack of a better term, this 1ˢᵗ-century Cambodian kingdom will be forever known as the Kingdom of Funan.

The Kingdom of Funan was situated around the Mekong River in a region made up of a good chunk of what's called Indochina—the peninsula that juts off the mainland of Southeast Asia. It lies east of

India and south of China, and for centuries, it has been influenced by these two giants of Asia.

Initially, the people of Funan were made up of loosely connected communities, each with its own leader. Eventually, these communities fused together under one centralized administration to form a much more powerful kingdom. Important trade routes were established between China and India by the 2nd century, making Cambodia a vital crossroads between the two regions. It was through increased traffic with India that Indian religion, culture, and writing styles began to take root in Cambodia.

Sanskrit writing, in particular, became the glue that held Cambodian intellectual thought together. Sanskrit was the foundation of written languages in Southeast Asia, much like how the Latin alphabet became the main basis of writing across Europe. The subsequent language that developed would become known as "Khmer," but the early lettering of this language was achieved through a variation of Sanskrit.

The Kingdom of Funan was at its most powerful in the 3rd century when it was governed by King Fan Shih-man, a ruler whose realm stretched toward Burma in the west, Malaysia in the south, Vietnam in the east, and Laos in the north. Under the leadership of King Fan Shih-man, the Cambodians were able to beef up their naval power and institute a streamlined bureaucratic government over their growing kingdom. This system forged a loose confederation of local regions under a centralized authority, which managed to keep the regions together without being too burdensome to the specific traditions and local governance of the various regional rulers.

Through its adoption of Sanskrit and Indian religious and legal practices, it is said that the powerful Kingdom of Funan helped to rapidly spread these same ideas all across Southeast Asia. The Kingdom of Funan continued to grow over the next few centuries, but it would eventually be overrun by a new southeastern powerhouse called the Chenla Kingdom. Chenla was initially a vassal state of Funan, but over the years, this former vassal grew powerful enough to challenge Funan itself.

Not a whole lot is known about this period of Cambodian history, and most of the written records we do have relies heavily on Chinese historians from the time. At any rate, the Chenla Kingdom began to decline by the late 7th century, and by 706 CE, Chenla had been divided into two major polities—one in the north known as Upper Chenla and one in the south called Lower Chenla.

Sometime around the 8th century, Lower Chenla was absorbed into nearby Java's powerful Shailendra dynasty as a subservient satellite. However, none of the local Cambodian powerbrokers were prepared for the rise of the next big boys on the block—the Khmer Empire. The Khmer Empire came into being when a man named Jayavarman II rose to prominence and began to lead military strikes against the subservient vassal states of Southeast Asia. He was quite successful in his campaigns, and soon, he was in control of a large swath of territory.

As his fame and power increased, Jayavarman II took on the name "Chakravartin," which translates as "Universal Ruler." King Jayavarman II created a dynasty of what were known as "devarajas," or "god-kings." As the name implies, it was believed that these rulers had been anointed by the powers of heaven to rule over their subjects. Although King Jayavarman II ruled through a policy of "might makes right," it seems that he was a fairly stabilizing ruler. He also managed to bring several principalities under his dominion just as much through political wheeling and dealing as he did through the use of the sword.

Jayavarman II moved the seat of governance to the inland regions of Cambodia's Tonle Sap Lake, founding a capital that would become known as Angkor. Jayavarman II passed away nearly fifty years after the founding of his empire, and after he died, the torch was passed to his son, Jayavarman III. Not much is known about the reign of Jayavarman III, but since there were no major upheavals during this period, it seems that he must have ruled his kingdom well enough. Upon his passing, the throne was then taken by his cousin, Indravarman I.

Indravarman ruled for a little over a decade before he died, passing the reins over to his son, Yasovarman I. Yasovarman invested heavily in the city of Yasodharapura, which would eventually be named Angkor. Some of the longest-lasting fixtures of this king's legacy were the large water reservoirs he implemented in order to take advantage of the region's natural water supply. There are a few inscriptions referencing this king, but they are fairly mythic in scope.

One inscription, for example, states that Yasovarman was "a giant capable of wrestling with elephants and slaying tigers with his bare hands." All of that elephant wrestling must have taken its toll, however, as the great king eventually passed away in 910 after ruling for around twenty-one years. After his demise, his eldest son, Harshavarman, took over. He ruled for some twenty-two years, and he seemed to have reigned over a prosperous kingdom. In fact, an inscription dated to the end of his reign in 922 documents the heavy tax revenue brought in from rice. Known as the Tuol Pei inscription, this artifact is interesting because it makes special mention of how certain religious groups had been deemed tax-exempt. Like in any governing body, taxes were important, but certain religious institutions apparently benefited from this tax-exempt status. At any rate, when Harshavarman died, he passed the baton to his little brother, Isanavarman II.

Isanavarman II's administration was a brief one; it is believed it lasted for around five years. In 928, he was toppled by Jayavarman IV. This king would rule for around thirteen years. Jayavarman IV engaged in many construction projects during his reign, and he wasn't above using slave labor to accomplish his ends. This is evidenced in an official inscription from Jayavarman IV's reign, which records the king ordering some 117 slaves for construction work on a couple of his temples.

Jayavarman IV was followed by Harshavarman II, who only ruled for just two years before Rajendravarman II arrived on the scene in 944. Rajendravarman was yet another temple builder, and under his steady hand, several more religious facilities were constructed, among them the famed Pre Rup temple, which still stands to this day. The Pre Rup temple was built in dedication to the Hindu deity Shiva, and it consists of three levels. It was largely lost to history until French archaeologists stumbled upon the structure in the 1930s. It had been literally buried by the sands of time, but after a careful excavation, much of it was found to still be intact. The structure is said to be representative of Mount Meru—a symbolic feature in the Hindu religion and a theme that can be found throughout Cambodia's ancient Hindu temples.

Out of all of the potentates to grace Angkor, by far one of the most important was Suryavarman II, who reigned from 1113 to 1150. Under Suryavarman II, the kingdom would extend from Cambodia into Vietnam and southern Laos. Eventually, even Thailand would become a vassal state to this powerful ruler. But his most lasting legacy, by far, was the construction of the grand temple complex in the capital city of Angkor known as Angkor Wat. Angkor Wat, which spans across some 400 acres, is the most expansive religious-themed monument on the planet. And the people who built it realized just how big their religious monument was, as indicated by the fact that they named it "Angkor Wat," which actually translates into English as "Temple City."

The fact is, under the rule of Suryavarman II, there was no such thing as separation of church and state. Thus, this "Temple City" was the heart of all political happenings in the empire. Although Angkor Wat was later converted into a religious site for Buddhism, it was originally created in reverence of Hinduism. Indeed, it was supposed to represent Mount Meru, the Hindu center of the universe. And even after Suryavarman II passed, the temple complex was still used for Hindu practice, as was indicated by an inscription made in the temple in his honor. The sacred inscription contained the term

Paramavishnuloka, which means "He who has entered the heavenly world of Vishnu."

Early Cambodians were indeed dedicated to the religion of Hinduism. This is a religion that Westerners often misinterpret to be polytheistic when, in reality, it is monotheistic. Yes, Hinduism on the surface appears to have hundreds of deities in a pantheon just as robust as ancient Greece, but what many fail to realize is that the gods of Hinduism are believed to be merely multiple manifestations of the one true god called Brahma. In fact, Hindus could be just as easily classified as believers of pantheism since they believe that all of us—me, you, Shiva, Vishnu, a cat, a dog, or even a rock—are all merely manifestations of the same super consciousness/god. While in our separate forms, we may feel that we are separate and distinct entities, in reality, we are just pieces of the same whole. We are made up of the same original energy/god essence that permeates all of creation. Or, as the sacred Vedas of Hinduism proclaim, "Everything is Brahmin." Angkor Wat was built to serve as a testament to this belief system.

In Angkor Wat's memorial to the dead king Suryavarman II, there is an elaborate depiction of how the god-king allegedly merged with Vishnu upon his passing. Hindus believe that when we die, all of our fractured and split consciousnesses, after so many periods of reincarnations/rebirths, will ultimately merge back together. This will ultimately lead to the eventual return to the source of it all—Brahma. If a Hindu were to have a near-death experience and see a bright light at the end of a tunnel, beckoning them to become part of it, they would no doubt assume this to be their consciousness merging back with Brahma, the origin of where it came from in the first place.

Along with being a religious site, Angkor Wat was also a kind of scientific outpost, especially in regards to astronomy. These discoveries have only recently come to light, but it turns out that Angkor Wat was built with an amazing sense of precision, as it seems the massive complex was made into a platform for observing the heavens. Many

Hindu mystics and ancient astronomers alike must have spent many hours in quiet contemplation as they scanned the heavens.

The original construction of the complex is shrouded in mystery. Back in the 13th century, a visiting Chinese diplomat was regaled with the tale that the complex was not built by human hands but rather a divine entity who erected the complex in a "single night." However, even those skeptical of Angkor Wat's supposed divine origins have to admit that it was an incredible feat of engineering.

A Portuguese friar named António da Madalena paid a visit to the complex in 1586, and he was awed by what he bore witness to. António described Angkor Wat as being an "extraordinary construction." He even insisted that the sight of it was so incredible that he was unable to "describe it with a pen." However, he tried his best, reporting back to his handlers in Portugal that Angkor Wat "is like no other building in the world. It has towers and decoration and all the refinements which the human genius can conceive of." He then went on to state, "There are many smaller towers of similar style, in the same stone, which are gilded. The temple is surrounded by a moat, and access is by a single bridge, protected by two stone tigers so grand and fearsome as to strike terror into the visitor."

Just two decades after the death of King Suryavarman II, the capital city of Angkor was invaded by the Cham people of southern Vietnam. Angkor Wat itself was ultimately sacked by these invaders in 1177. Despite the "grand and fearsome" visages of the stone sentinels that António later reported on, these intruders apparently wasted no time in seizing control of the temple complex.

The Khmer and Cham peoples have had a long history of warfare with each other. In the year 1177, Cham forces, who were said to have been guided by a Chinese diplomat who had previously visited the city, set sail on the mighty Mekong, making their way to the great Tonle Sap, where they then proceeded to storm Angkor itself. As dramatic as this offensive was, it proved to be a very short-lived victory. After the forces of the Khmer Empire rallied, the invaders were sent running back to the Kingdom of Champa from whence they had come.

This blatant assault proved to be a great political coup for the rulers of the Khmer Empire in the meantime, as it gave them more than enough reason to launch a bloody crusade against the Chams. This resulted in Champa itself becoming a subservient satellite of the Khmer Empire. But even so, the fact that the capital of this great realm had been struck led many of the Khmer elite to question how such a thing could have occurred in the first place. It was in the midst of all of this questioning that a new king—Jayavarman VII—came to power and decided to change the state religion from Hinduism to Buddhism.

Jayavarman VII was said to have been a rather compassionate ruler as it pertained to his subjects. In fact, he was famous for establishing so-called "hospital temples" in which the average citizen could have ailments cared for. Seeming to bear testament to this altruism and concern for the general welfare of the public is a 12th-century inscription about the king at one of these hospitals, which reads, "He suffered the illnesses of his subjects more than his own; because it is the pain of the public that is the pain of kings rather than their own pain."

In light of the Cham invasion, which was followed by fierce warfare with the Cham and then the adoption of Buddhism, the Khmer Empire was going through some rather significant changes. In reality, Hinduism and Buddhism had coexisted to some extent for hundreds of years. But it was Jayavarman VII who became the first king of the Khmer Empire who established Buddhism as the official, preferred religion of the state. This religious shift was similar in scope to when Emperor Constantine of the Roman Empire tolerated and then made Christianity the official religion of the realm in the 4th century.

Thus, in a similar fashion, in the 12th century, Jayavarman VII set the stage for this great transition from the old religion of Hinduism to the newly accepted religion of Buddhism. Although there is no way to know for certain, it is believed that the Cham invasion and the subsequent desecration of the Hindu temple city may have had something to do with it. It could be that this shocking incident led to a loss of belief in the Khmer kings being a manifestation of the invincible Hindu deity. Instead, many began to turn to what seemed to be the more pragmatic Buddhism, which made sense of the recent pain and suffering of the kingdom. After all, the main thrust of Buddhism is its quest to relieve suffering.

This more compassionate bent led King Jayavarman VII to not only secure the borders of the empire but to also greatly improve living conditions within those borders. It was under Jayavarman VII, after all, that some of the greatest infrastructure projects of the Khmer Empire were made. This included new roadways, dams, reservoirs, and, of course, the countless temple hospitals dedicated to the healing and general well-being of the populace. These hospitals were way ahead of their time, and they offered spiritual prayers as well as medicinal herbs for the sick and infirm. At any rate, this great stage of civilization in Cambodia would come to a close in the first half of the 1400s. By then, the Khmer Empire was suffering a great decline while other forces in the region were ready to expand.

Chapter 3 – The Rise of the Kingdom of Vietnam

"Throughout the 20th century, the Republican Party benefited from a non-interventionist foreign policy. Think of how Eisenhower came in to stop the Korean War. Think of how Nixon was elected to stop the mess in Vietnam."

-Ron Paul

It is hard to argue against the notion that when people hear of the nation of Vietnam today, they first think of the quagmire that was the Vietnam War, a conflict that pitted communist Vietnamese forces against US troops. But Vietnam, of course, has a rich history that took root long before Marxism was ever in vogue. In fact, the Vietnamese civilization is said to have first flowered in approximately 2500 BCE.

These early Vietnamese settlements, like many of their neighbors, relied heavily on the farming of rice fields. As the settlements became more prosperous and the population increased, local landlords rose up to consolidate their power. This led to a kind of feudal confederacy that remained in place until the much more cohesive civilization of China decided to invade during the 2nd century BCE.

Although southern Vietnam remained largely out of China's reach, the Chinese would be the masters of northern Vietnam for over 1,000 years. However, China's grip on North Vietnam was a tenuous one, and periodic rebellions staged by homegrown Vietnamese insurgencies during this span of time were quite commonplace. The Vietnamese became experts at guerilla warfare in their struggle against the Chinese—a skill that would be realized once again in their 20th-century struggle for self-determination.

However, as it pertains to the Vietnamese struggle against China, things came to a head in 939 CE when Vietnamese forces managed to overthrow Chinese rule once and for all. It was one of the victorious Vietnamese generals—Ngo Quyen—who would become the first Vietnamese ruler of the independent Kingdom of Vietnam, which consisted of modern-day North and Central Vietnam.

King Ngo Quyen reigned for just five years before perishing, and his death sent the Kingdom of Vietnam into a terrible internal war of succession known as the "upheaval of the Twelve Warlords." It was called as such because, in the vacuum of clear leadership, a war was waged by twelve powerful warlords who controlled twelve different regions of Vietnam. The powerful Vietnamese General Dinh Bo Linh eventually wrested control over the twelve warlords in 968 CE, bringing all of Vietnam under his authority in the process.

It must be noted, however, that even with an attempt at centralized control, North Vietnam was always markedly different from South Vietnam. Ever since the start of the Chinese occupation, North Vietnam had become culturally and administratively more Chinese in character than South Vietnam. South Vietnam had become the wild, untamed land of the Cham people, while the North Vietnamese had much more in common with the Han Chinese.

At any rate, when Dinh Bo Linh seized control, it marked the beginning of the Vietnamese Dinh dynasty. The dynasty established by General Dinh would hit a bump in the road in 979 when the emperor,

Dinh Bo Linh, who, upon his coronation, was given the name Dinh Tien Hoang, and the crown prince, Dinh Lien, were both assassinated. This left Emperor Hoang's six-year-old son Dinh Toan (who would be given the title of Dinh Phe De) as the heir. Since a six-year-old is obviously not going to be able to rule by themself, this meant that court officials had to rule through the child.

It was during this period of instability that China's Song dynasty decided to launch a renewed attempt to take Vietnam back as a subservient state. Chinese forces swooped down on North Vietnam in 979. At the onset of this crisis, the great Vietnamese general Le Hoan took over the leadership of the nation. Le Hoan proved himself to be an ingenious leader, and although the odds were stacked against his kingdom, he found ways to offset the more powerful Chinese forces through the use of his brilliant tactics.

Since the smaller Vietnamese military would never be able to face the larger Chinese army, Le Hoan developed a scheme in which he lured the Chinese troops to cross into the narrow confines of Chi Lang Pass. This proved fatal for the Chinese army since it enabled the Vietnamese to systematically pick off the Chinese soldiers while they were hemmed in by the rock walls of the mountain pass. This terrible defeat sent the Chinese packing and reasserted the strength of northern Vietnam.

The northern Vietnamese, in the meantime, began to steadily expand their territory into southern Vietnam, encroaching upon the territory of the Kingdom of Champa. Le Hoan, who had taken the title of "Emperor Le Dai Hanh," died in 1005 CE, and he was succeeded by his son, Le Trung Tong, who ruled for an impressive three days before dying. His brother, Le Long Dinh, also known as Le Ngoa Trieu, proved to be a cruel dictator, but his terrible reign didn't last long, although it was longer than his brother's—he passed away just a few years later in 1009.

After this tyrant's death, the Vietnamese court made what was probably a wise decision by bypassing any hereditary claims to the throne and handing power over to a humble but capable military general by the name of Ly Cong Uan, who would begin the powerful Ly dynasty. One of the first major moves of Ly Cong Uan, whose regnal name was Ly Thai To, was to establish a new capital for his kingdom in what we now call Hanoi.

The Ly dynasty is known for its complex bureaucracy, which was very similar to China's, in which government officials could be trained and officiated through the undertaking of government-sponsored exams. The Kingdom of Vietnam also developed a modern system of taxation, which was used to keep the government apparatus functioning. As for the religion of the kingdom, both Buddhism and a variation of Taoism reigned supreme.

But despite all of this headway, China's Song dynasty was not quite ready to let the Kingdom of Vietnam go. In 1075, it launched yet another assault upon North Vietnam. The Vietnamese were ready, and knowing that an invasion was about to be launched, they actually struck out at the Chinese first, launching devastating attacks against Chinese military mobilizations in the regions of Guangxi and Guangdong.

The Song dynasty itself would then be subjected to invasion by the mighty Jurchen Jin, who defeated the Song military in northern China in 1126. The Jurchen Jin originally hailed from Manchuria, which was northeast of China proper. They would go on to found an empire that would include northern China, Mongolia, and much of Korea.

This major event led the government of the Song dynasty to relocate to southern China, where a new government was established in Hangzhou. The Song dynasty would never again attempt a major military strike against North Vietnam, and it would be completely extinguished by an invading Mongol horde led by the successor of Genghis Khan: the famous Kublai Khan. The Mongol campaign began in 1260, and it ended in 1276 with the capture of Hangzhou, followed by the city of Canton, where the last holdouts of the Song government of southern China were holed up.

With the Mongols in control of China, it wasn't long before they turned their attention to China's southeastern borders and began plotting to take over Vietnam as well. Soon, the Mongols led their forces, along with Chinese troops and naval power, to engage in an assault on northern Vietnam. The Vietnamese, who were by now well versed in defensive warfare, were able to repel the invaders, and the Mongol forces failed in their endeavors. Faced with numerically superior forces, the Vietnamese repeated the same tactics that they had used against the Song dynasty in which they kept the enemy at bay without getting lured into open engagements, as they knew their smaller forces would have been crushed.

North Vietnam also temporarily aligned with the Champa Kingdom of South Vietnam, presenting a united front to the aggressors. The Mongols, meanwhile, who had become stretched entirely too thin, soon had to retreat back to higher ground. Once the Mongol threat had been removed, North Vietnam and South Vietnam began to do battle with each other, as the Kingdom of Vietnam once again began to expand into Champa territory in the south.

These efforts resulted in the Champa Kingdom being reduced to a vassal state of the Kingdom of Vietnam in 1312. But after just a decade, the Champa Kingdom was able to break free, resulting in a war that would last three decades. Very little was gained out of this conflict, and the Kingdom of Vietnam was so weakened that it invited a fresh invasion from China in 1407.

China, by this time, had shaken off its Mongol overlords. Thus, it was the Ming dynasty that sought to make the Kingdom of Vietnam a client state once again. The Vietnamese had known independence for far too long to take this attempted subjugation lying down. By the 1420s, the Vietnamese were launching massive rebellions against Chinese authority. The Ming forces were ultimately defeated in 1426, thereby ending the last attempt by China to directly exert control over Vietnam.

The brief Ming occupation was in many ways more beneficial to North Vietnam than it was detrimental. After all, it was the Ming who introduced siege weapons, such as canons and gunpowder, and other technological innovations, such as the printing press and paper, to the North Vietnamese.

In 1471, a resurgent North Vietnam was able to march on Champa and seized most of the former Champa territory, incorporating it into the greater Vietnam. The destruction of the Champa Kingdom kicked off a diaspora of the Cham people, who moved to other neighboring regions of Southeast Asia. By 1479, the Kingdom of Vietnam had also expanded into Laos, leading to what has been called the Vietnamese-Laotian War. The war ended in 1484 in what was essentially a draw between the two regional powers, as neither side gained much of anything for their efforts.

Over the next few decades, the Kingdom of Vietnam began to deteriorate steadily due to a wide range of factors. These factors included political turmoil, economic distress, and climate change having an adverse effect on agricultural output. With all of these problems, Vietnamese expansion seemed to be at an end. It was right around this time when Vietnam began to shrink back that the outside world came knocking.

Chapter 4 –Thailand and Its Early Kingdoms

"When I was first lady, I worked to call attention to the plight of refugees fleeing Cambodia for Thailand. I visited Thailand and witnessed firsthand the trauma of parents and children separated by circumstances beyond their control."

-Former First Lady Rosalynn Carter

The history of Thailand is one that frequently merges and blends with its neighbors of southern China, Burma, Malaysia, Cambodia, and Vietnam, which all played a major role in the shaping of Thailand. The name "Thailand" itself is derived from the "Tai people." The Tais in ancient times referred to their kingdom as simply "Meuang Thai," which, roughly translated, means "Land of the Tais."

It is believed that the Tai ethnic and linguistic group originated in southern China. Around the year 700 CE, a significant portion of Tais came to live in what now constitutes the modern-day city of Dien Bien Phu in northern Vietnam. These Tais would then gradually move southwest, following the local waterways that would lead them deeper into the territory of what is now Thailand. But just because the Tais made the region their home, that does not mean they were the first to lay claim to the land.

According to a piece of traditional Tai folklore called the Simhanavati legend, the region was first inhabited by the Wa people before the mighty King Simhanavati of the Tais led a brutal assault against them and forced them to flee. This led to the founding of the Tai settlement of Chiang Saen in 800 CE. Soon after this, the Tais of the region developed relationships with their "Indianized" neighbors and began to practice Buddhism. They also developed a form of Sanskrit writing.

All was relatively peaceful for the next few decades, but by 900 CE, war had erupted between the Tais of Chiang Saen and the neighboring Mons of Burma. The war ended up being fairly devastating for the Tais, as their capital was overrun and sacked by the Mons. It wasn't until 937 that the Tais were able to rally their forces and drive the Mons out of the region. However, the Tais would receive another blow in 1000 CE when a major earthquake tore right through Chiang Saen.

This earthquake was devastating, as it leveled the city and left many dead. The situation was so dire that the inhabitants enacted what today we might call a state of emergency, as they instituted a special council just to maintain order. Fortunes would improve enough by 1100, and the Tais would begin to expand their kingdom to the south. As the Tais expanded to the south, they came into contact with Cambodia's Khmer people and began to be heavily influenced by the Khmer culture.

By the early 1200s, Thailand would reach what would be considered its "golden age." By the time the Khmer Empire began to wane, the first major Thai kingdom would emerge. It was in approximately 1240 CE that Pho Khun Bang Klang was made the first ruler of what would become known as the Sukhothai Kingdom. The kingdom was called as such because it was based around the Thai settlement of Sukhothai in central Thailand. This particular Thai kingdom was known to be one filled with rich resources, as it was said to have had an abundance of fresh fish and rice paddies.

During this period, the Thais had peaceful relations with their neighbors, both abroad and at home. In fact, to ensure this sense of peace and tranquility, it is said that if there was any problem, all a resident had to do was ring a bell that was installed right outside of the king's palace, and he would arrive on the scene to settle the dispute. If such accounts are accurate, it must have been surely used as a subject's final recourse over a major disturbance. One has to imagine the king would probably get frustrated fairly quickly if his people were bugging him over every single petty squabble that might erupt.

At any rate, the king was seen by the Thais as a kind of fatherly figure who had their best interests at heart. One of the most memorable kings to rule during this period was the Thai potentate Ram Khamhaeng, who served as the head of the kingdom from 1279 to 1298. Archaeological evidence of his reign has been uncovered in the form of the so-called "Ram Khamhaeng Stele," which is a kind of "inscribed tablet" that commemorates the king's rule. In keeping with the paternalistic nature of the kingship, the stele describes Ram Khamhaeng as a fatherly king who cared deeply for his people. There is no doubt that Ram Khamhaeng certainly was a great and powerful king with a lasting influence. In fact, it is said that he may have been the one who actually established the Thai alphabet. After all, it was on his stele that this script was first seen to be in use.

Another important Thai leader was Maha Thammaracha I, who came to power around the year 1347. Maha Thammaracha established Theravada Buddhism as the main religion of the realm. Theravada Buddhism is essentially orthodox Buddhism, meaning that it was the first main school of Buddhist thought to emerge. Buddhism began in India, but it subsequently spread throughout Asia. As the teachings of the Buddha spread, different branches emerged. By the time it fully reached as far as Japan, for example, the Japanese had developed a variation called Zen Buddhism. Those believing in Theravada Buddhism are originalists, so they reject these later variations. Although the religion originated in India, which was is also the land of Hinduism, Buddhism rejects much of Hindu belief. Buddhism would never quite catch on in its place of birth, but it would spread to India's neighbors in East and Southeast Asia.

Buddhism itself is a unique religion in the sense that it is a religious practice that is not centered around a deity. Buddhists do not believe in a god—they simply acknowledge that a cosmic force exists and that it runs through nature. As such, Buddhism does not focus on pleasing a god as much as it focuses on finding a way to live a virtuous and enlightened life through philosophical concepts, such as the "Middle Way," "The Four Noble Truths," and "The Noble Eightfold Path." By reaching enlightenment, a Buddhist believes that one can break the cycle of rebirth and suffering and reach a state of Nirvana. The Buddha himself is said to have been someone who "awakened" to this ultimate truth. After doing so, he sought to bestow this understanding upon the rest of humanity through his teachings. The Buddha basically taught that we are all trapped in our own false narratives of suffering but can learn to free ourselves from them. Theravada Buddhists furthermore believe that every so often, an enlightened one like the Buddha emerges in order to help the rest of us wake up from the vicious cycle that we are trapped in.

At any rate, it was around the time of Maha Thammaracha that the Thai Ayutthaya Kingdom arose. This dynastic kingdom would last the longest, staying in existence all the way until 1767. During this period, the kingdom of Thailand became an economic powerhouse, taking advantage of its position between several powerful states to become a major trading partner in the region. But as the power of the kingdom grew, the rights of its citizens lessened. Whereas in the past, any subject could ring a bell and state their grievance to the king as equals, during the Ayutthaya Kingdom, there was a clear class distinction. The kings were all powerful, and they were perceived as having essentially a mandate from heaven to do whatever they wished, which, by the way, is definitely not something encouraged by Buddhist belief. Nevertheless, by the 15th century, the Ayutthaya Kingdom was powerful enough to even take on the Khmer Empire, and it is said to have bested their Khmer neighbors in battle on three separate occasions.

During the 1500s, another Thai kingdom called Lanna existed in the north. These two kingdoms would intermittently wage war with each other until the Lanna Kingdom fell to the neighboring Burma kingdom in 1558. The Ayutthaya Kingdom, in the meantime, came into contact with visitors from outside of Southeast Asia entirely when the Portuguese arrived in the region in 1511. Soon after contacts with the Portuguese were made, the French began to take an interest in the region as well. For a while, the feeling seemed to be mutual. King Narai of Ayutthaya, in particular, who reigned from 1656 to 1688, developed close ties with King Louis XIV of France. As the relationship grew, the Ayutthayan king allowed French missionaries to his realm and even installed French soldiers for the kingdom's national defense.

However, this foreign influence led to much dissent and unrest in the king's court. This unrest would continue to grow until it erupted in what would become known as the Siamese revolution of 1688. For it was this year that a popular revolt broke out against the king, which led to his overthrow. The revolt was led by a Thai general named Phetracha, who deposed the king, seized the throne for himself, and drove out the French. The most dramatic moment of this revolution was during the so-called Siege of Bangkok. Bangkok had become a prosperous port city by this time, and the French had some 200 of their troops holed up in a fortress. Some 40,000 Thai troops were said to have waged an assault on this fort, but the French were able to hold them off long enough to negotiate a deal that would allow them to evacuate the city. This move would effectively isolate Thailand from the

Western world until Western interests would once again intrude upon the land of the Thais in the 1800s.

Chapter 5: The Political Intrigue of Ancient Indonesia

"Think Indonesia and tourism, and the first thing that comes to mind is probably Bali. Think golf holiday, and most people would dream of Scotland or Ireland. But Indonesia harbors one of the best-kept secrets in the world of travel: it is a golfer's paradise."

-Raymond Bonner

Indonesia is a thriving nation in Southeast Asia filled with a rich and vibrant history. Like many regions of Southeast Asia, Indonesia owes much of its ancient heritage to the subcontinent of India. The name itself, in fact, comes from the Greek appellation of *Indos Nesos*, which literally means "Indonesia." Indian religion and culture were prevalent in Indonesia as early as 200 BCE.

It is around this time that the Indian epic *Ramayana* was written. And within this ancient Sanskrit text, there is mention of a great kingdom called "Yawadvipa" located on the Indonesian island of Java. Not a whole lot can be drawn from this narrative, but it definitely indicates that Java was a known quantity at the very least. Today, Java is the most populated island on the planet, and it holds the bustling Indonesian metropolis of Jakarta.

However, back in 200 BCE, it's not entirely clear what the ancient Indonesian kingdom of Java might have been like, but it was at least noteworthy enough for Indian scribes to mention it in one of their epic narratives. Ancient Indonesia also had close political and mercantile ties with both India and China. Since the islands were positioned between these two Asian powerhouses, Indonesia would have been a valuable weigh station. Some trade, such as Indonesia's extensive export of cloves, traveled far and wide, with this precious Indonesian spice having appeared as far afield as ancient Rome.

Roman historian Pliny the Elder made mention of Indonesian crafts making their way to ports in East Africa, where they undoubtedly then made their way north to Egypt and then across the Mediterranean to Rome itself. The Indonesians had such a presence in the region that it is believed they may have even had a settlement on the island of Madagascar. The Indonesians were indeed a great seafaring people during this time, and there are independent sources that back this up.

For instance, according to the modern-day author and Southeast Asia researcher Colin Brown, there are Chinese records from sometime around 300 CE that speak of the Indonesians having large trading vessels that were as long as 50 meters (164 feet), which would have been loaded with all kinds of precious goods and commodities. It was only once the Roman Empire went into decline in the 4th century that Indonesians began to turn back to primarily trade in East and Southeast Asia.

After this pivotal shift, Indonesia began to transform from a trading outpost and weigh station into a dynamic political entity in its own right. The first known kingdom was centered around the island of Java, and it was called Tarumanegara. This kingdom was ruled by a king named Purnawarman, whose reign has been verified through inscribed stones dating back to 450 CE. Not a lot is known about the kings that immediately came after Purnawarman, but by 535 CE, another powerful ruler by the name of Suryawarman (not to be confused with

Suryavarman I—the Cambodian king) seems to have emerged. Suryawarman set up a new capital and established the kingdom of Sunda Sambawa.

Here, the records get a bit murky, and the next we know of Indonesian governance is the kingdom of Ho-Ling, which comes down to us from Chinese sources dating back to 640. As you might have guessed, "Ho-Ling" is actually a Chinese name, and it is most likely not what the actual residents called their kingdom. Some believe that the name is actually a Chinese attempt to pronounce the Indonesian word "Kalingga." At any rate, the Chinese called the place Ho-ling, and that is the name that stuck for this epoch of Indonesian history. According to the Chinese, the ruler of Ho-Ling entered into contact with the Chinese for the purpose of trade, which means Ho-Ling superseded Tarumanegara as the main ambassador kingdom of Indonesia.

As well as being steeped in the mercantile business of trade goods, Ho-Ling was also quite blessed when it came to developing productive farms. During this period, rice production was quite abundant, and the people not only grew enough to keep the locals well nourished but also to have plenty of leftover products to sell to other nations.

Contact between China and Indonesia during this time was quite strong. By the 670s, the Chinese were even sending Buddhist missionaries to the region. This was the case in December of 671 when a Chinese monk by the name of Yijing left Yanjing (modern-day Beijing) and made his way to the Indonesian island of Sumatra at a town that Yijing called Sanfoqi. The locale was actually the city of Srivijaya. This bustling port city would soon become the capital of a powerful mercantile state based out of the Indonesian island of Sumatra. Upon coming ashore, Yijing made his way to the local raja's headquarters. It was then arranged for him to meet the king, who is said to have taken kindly to the Chinese monk and helped facilitate his Buddhist activities while in the region.

Yijing, as much as he was ready to spread the gospel of Buddhism, was pleasantly surprised that the religion had already taken root on the island. Yijing would later record in his journal, "In the fortified city of Fo-Qi [Srivijaya], Buddhist priests number more than one thousand, whose minds are bent on learning and good practices. They investigate and study all the subjects that exist just as in [India]; the rules and ceremonies are not at all different. If a Chinese priest wishes to go to the West in order to listen and read, he had better stay here one or two years and practice the proper rules and then proceed to central India." Buddhism, of course, originated in India, and when Yijing speaks of going to "the West," he means going west from China to Indonesia and then ultimately on to India itself, which Yijing did himself in December of 672.

Once again, Indonesia was being considered as a weigh station, but this time for religion. The kingdom of Ho-Ling was predominantly Buddhist, but as was and still is the case with most religious factions in Indonesia, this predominant strain was built upon an ancient ancestral religion that heavily influenced the region's variations of religious practices.

Srivijaya, in the meantime, became the seat of a powerful confederation of port cities that were all heavily involved in the trade economy. By the early 700s, this confederacy was essentially a mini-empire with Srivijaya as its seat of power. During this time, Chinese records officially acknowledge the region as a vassal state, recording regular tribute passing from the Srivijayan leader to the emperor of China. But by the middle of the 8th century, the Srivijayan kingdom began to be overshadowed by another Indonesian kingdom, whose name has come down to us as Mataram.

The polity of Mataram would construct some of the first monasteries on the islands of Indonesia, with some of the greatest being situated just north of the Indonesian metropolis of Yogyakarta. In fact, it was near Yogyakarta that the grandest Buddhist temple of them all—Borobudur—

was built. This colossal structure is said to have cost quite a bit of money to pay the many hands who helped to construct it. And since this religious edifice had no real monetary return—just spiritual ones—it's generally taken as a sign that Mataram must have been fairly well off to fund such a project in the first place.

Mataram picked up right where Ho-Ling had left off by controlling the mercantile trade of the region with big players such as China. Mataram was also quite successful in growing an abundant amount of rice, thereby ensuring enduring prosperity for the kingdom. The Srivijayan kingdom began to lose favor with China, and once the Chinese began to send their own merchants abroad, they didn't have as much use for the Srivijayans as trading partners. To make matters worse, in 1025, a group of South Indian pirates called the Cholas invaded and sacked the capital. After this assault, Srivijaya never quite recovered its former prestige as a trading hub in Indonesia. At any rate, just as Srivijaya was in decline, Mataram began to take off, and it would reach new heights of success under the leadership of a man named Airlangga.

From his capital of Surabaya, Airlangga held a monopoly over the trade of fine spices and rice production. In 1045, before he abdicated his throne, Airlangga divided his kingdom up between his two sons, with west Mataram being turned into a state called Kediri and east Mataram being rendered into a place called Janggala. Kediri had the better ports and thus proved to be the more capable province.

By the 1100s, subsequent rulers of Kediri had been able to successfully take over and reincorporate Janggala, creating a single powerful kingdom. In addition, they also made the regions of Kalimantan and Bali fall under their sway. However, after about a 100-year run, this expanded Kediri Kingdom would be overrun in 1222 when Ken Angrok of nearby Tumapel, in East Java, seized the territory for himself. Ken Angrok forged yet another capital, Singhasari, which was situated near the Kali Welang River Basin in the vicinity of the modern-day Indonesian city of Malang.

The last leader of this subsequent Javanese empire was a man named Kertanegara, who ruled from 1268 to 1292. During his reign, the Mongol warlord Kublai Khan began pressuring Indonesia to pay tribute to the Mongol Empire. Kertanegara refused to fork out the tribute and dismissed the khagan's representatives outright. This, of course, did not sit at all well with Kublai Khan, and in 1292, he made his displeasure known by way of a massive military invasion in which nearly a thousand ships and around 20,000 troops were sent to lay siege to Java.

However, if Kublai Khan wanted to exact vengeance on the insolent Kertanegara, he was too late. By the time this massive army arrived, Kertanegara was already dead. He had fallen victim to local political intrigue and was assassinated by a local prince by the name of Jayakatwang, who then declared himself king. By the time the Mongols arrived, they were briefed by the happenings and were persuaded to side with Kertanegara's son-in-law, Raden Vijaya, who was struggling to take the throne for himself.

Raden proved to be quite a crafty politician, and he soon would get the best of the Mongol horde. Initially, he won a diplomatic coup with the would-be invaders, as he actually managed to get them to agree to do battle with his enemy, Jayakatwang, the one responsible for Kertanegara's assassination. But as soon as the Mongols did his bidding and took out Jayakatwang, Raden turned his own forces on the Mongols. Not only that, but he also managed to develop a successful grassroots guerrilla warfare campaign in which all of his subjects were galvanized to annihilate the Mongols.

The bewildered Mongols, as fierce as they might have been, were just not prepared for this unexpected onslaught. With enemies assailing them on all sides in an unfamiliar and inhospitable land, they were ultimately forced to retreat. After successfully driving the Mongols off, Raden further consolidated his power and created a palace south of

Surabaya where he ruled and reigned supreme of a reconstituted Javanese empire that would become known as the Majapahit kingdom.

Raden Wijaya passed away in 1309, and he would be replaced by his own son, Jayanagara. However, Jayanagara would not fill his father's footsteps very well, and after amassing a scandalous reputation, he perished without an heir in 1328. This ushered in a period of dynastic instability with factions vying for power until the year 1350. In that year, a capable prince by the name of Hayam Wuruk, who just so happened to be the great-grandson of the murdered Kertanegara, made his way to the throne.

Under his steady hand, Majapahit would expand its reach to include Bali, Kalimantan, and Sumatra. During this time, both China and Europe were eager buyers of the spices that Indonesia had to offer, and the spice trade made the Majapahit kingdom quite rich. The Chinese and Europeans were using many of the Indonesian spices for both food seasoning and medicinal purposes.

As was usually the case during this period, it was China who began to pressure the Indonesians for extra perks and privileges when it came to trade. And after the Chinese managed to shake off the Mongols and establish the Ming dynasty in 1368, it wasn't long before China began to demand tribute in the form of favorable trade deals. By the early 1400s, China was sending regular expeditions to exact tribute from the Indonesians. In 1407, a Chinese delegation led by a famous member of the Ming court—Zheng He—found its way to the shores of Java. Zheng He found Majapahit to be a bustling land with a multitude of nationalities engaged in vibrant trade networks. However, it was a tad too rough for Zheng He's tastes, and his chroniclers would later report, among other things, that just about everyone had a knife and that they were all more than willing to use it.

This part of Southeast Asia would more or less lumber on in this same state of both cosmopolitan luxury and violent banditry for the next 100 or so years until new arrivals from farther afield would change the entire landscape of Indonesia for good.

Chapter 6 – Burma and the British

"This is Burma, and it will be quite unlike any land you know about."

-Rudyard Kipling

By the early 1800s, Burma and Britain seemed all but destined for a cataclysmic collision. At this point, Burma was in the middle of its last independent dynasty, that of the so-called Konbaung kings. It was the mighty King Bodawpaya who began to aggressively stab westward, as he took control of the fabled city of Arakan in 1785, which was then followed by the seizure of Manipur in 1814 and the acquisition of Assam in 1817. These territorial acquisitions brought the Burmese right to the border of what was then called British India.

Of course, this led to inevitable conflict and border skirmishes. In 1819, King Bodawpaya passed away and was succeeded by his grandson, Bagyidaw. King Bagyidaw proved to be even bolder than his grandfather and began to consider seizing the British-controlled territory of Bengal for himself. The British were well aware of the threat they faced, and wishing to weaken their competitors, they sought to sow seeds of chaos.

The British fanned the flames of dissent among residents of nearby Manipur and Assam during the early 1820s, hoping the territories would break away from the Konbaung dynasty and provide a more adequate buffer zone. However, the rebellions failed, so cross-border conflicts continued until the so-called First Anglo-Burmese War broke out in 1824.

In the first stage of the conflict, the British managed to catch the Burmese by surprise by striking directly against Lower Burma from a fleet of craft launched from the nearby Andaman Islands. The Burmese had been expecting a land invasion from the borderlands they shared with the British, but the Brits went right around the Burmese defenses and invaded by water. On May 10th, 1824, the British landed, and they managed to seize the strategic port city of Rangoon without much of a fight. This gave the British a toehold right inside Burmese territory, and now it was up to the Burmese to expel the British from their land.

From their perch in Rangoon, the British planned to travel up the Irrawaddy River to the capital of Burma itself. But soon after their arrival in Rangoon, they realized their invasion plans would be difficult as the wet and rainy monsoon season had begun, which made traveling upriver exceedingly difficult. Therefore, the British advance, which initially had much momentum on its side, stalled at Rangoon. The Brits ended up having to hole up for several months as they waited for the long, wet season to end. And throughout the monsoon season, their force, which initially numbered 11,000 strong, had been whittled down to less than a thousand combat-ready soldiers. This was largely due to the plagues of illness that had rocked the British, as they were not well adjusted to the tropical diseases of the region.

In the meantime, the Burmese forces, led by a general named Bandula, began to make their way to Rangoon with tens of thousands of troops and their best artillery in the hopes of driving the British out of Burma for good. Although the moribund and sickly British were stuck in Rangoon, they proved to be an intractable lot when defending the little piece of territory that they had captured. This can be seen in December of 1824 when the Burmese forces launched their assault on British-held Rangoon, as the Burmese were easily pushed back. Interestingly enough, this was the very same year that the British entered into the so-called Anglo-Dutch Treaty, which cut off part of the Malay Archipelago and affirmed British control over Singapore. During this period, Britain was most certainly on the rise when it came to the dominance of Southeast Asia.

At any rate, the British were able to easily cut through their assailants and cause great disorder. Faced with withering, relentless fire from the Brits, General Bandula was forced to call off the attack in fear that his whole army would fall apart. This victory seemed to rally the spirits of the British, and that spring, they finally left the protective confines of Rangoon and ventured toward the city of Prome.

In the skirmishes with the Burmese that followed, General Bandula lost his life, and his army retreated. This allowed the British to advance on Prome without much of a fight. These developments caused much distress to the Burmese king, as he quickly realized that things were not going at all well for the Burmese forces. Desperate to buy some time, the Burmese government reached out to the British and requested an armistice in the fall of 1825. However, these plans were scrapped when the British uncovered a Burmese scheme to take back Prome, and they left the bargaining table. The war would then rage on for much of the rest of 1825.

This same year, in neighboring Thailand, which was then known as Siam, the Siamese government was convinced to enter into a treaty with the British. This treaty saw Siam officially granting its recognition of British-controlled territory in Malaysia. In previous years, Siam had made some significant inroads into Malaysia, conquering the Kedah Sultanate in 1821. This put Siam in close proximity to British interests in the region. After seeing how easily the British were beating the

Burmese, the Kingdom of Siam was convinced that it would be in its own best interest to enter into diplomatic relations with the British rather than risk armed conflict. This move would ultimately prove to be beneficial to Thailand since it would remain the only Southeast Asian nation to remain independent and never be colonized by a European power.

However, Burma would not be so lucky. The war continued to go badly for the Burmese, and in time, both parties (the Burmese and the British) once again began negotiations. This time around, the British offered some pretty harsh terms for the Burmese to accept. They demanded that they be handed the territories of Arakan, Assam, Manipur, and Tenasserim, as well as be paid a hefty amount of rupees for their trouble.

As can be expected, the Burmese were enraged at these demands and immediately refused further negotiations. But once the British captured the city of Yandabo, which was not far from the Burmese capital itself, the Burmese began singing a different tune. Knowing that they didn't have much room to bargain, they finally agreed to the terms given to them by the British in a desperate bid to stave off complete collapse. This fear is what led the Burmese to sign the so-called Treaty of Yandabo on February 24th, 1826.

Forcing the Burmese to give up strategic territories such as Arakan, Asam, and Manipur gave the British the breathing room they desired, but now, Burma was just a shadow of what it had been. The kingdom was also heavily burdened by having to pay the British Crown reparations for the cost of the war. This was a humiliation for Burma and, in particular, for the Burmese king, Bagyidaw. It has been said that after this terrible defeat, King Bagyidaw spiraled into a full-blown depression that would haunt him for the rest of his life. In fact, things would get so bad at times that the queen and her family would often have to step in as stewards of the Burmese government while King Bagyidaw spent time recovering from his mental afflictions.

This stewardship was not looked upon favorably by Tharrawaddy Min, the king's younger brother. Tharrawaddy was disgusted by his brother's inability to rule, and he also didn't appreciate his brother's wife and family members stepping in for him. Deciding to put matters into his own hands, Tharrawaddy launched a coup in 1837, and he managed to knock his brother out of power and take his place as king of Burma.

Tharrawaddy Min was determined to reverse his sibling's losses, so he began to engage in wanton saber-rattling against the British. He also began cutting ties with British diplomats, and in the fall of 1841, he sent his forces to Rangoon in what was tantamount to a military parade in order to drive home his ambition to push the British out by force if need be. But despite all of this bravado, Tharrawaddy proved himself to be every bit as unstable as his older brother had been, and after several bouts of mental instability, his own sons had him locked away in 1845.

King Tharrawaddy Min passed away in 1846, paving the way for his son, Pagan Min, to take his place. However, relations between the British and the Burmese would break down once again. In 1851, the governor of Pegu Province took two British sea captains into custody for trumped-up charges of homicide, causing relations to hit an all-time low. The British predictably demanded the repatriation of its citizens, and when the Burmese government refused, the British sent its forces into Pegu in 1852, kickstarting what would become the Second Anglo-Burmese War.

The British ended up annexing Pegu that December. In the meantime, the Burmese court had begun to fear a complete collapse of the government, and in order to stave off utter annihilation, Burmese officials launched a coup against Pagan Min. After Pagan Min was removed from power, his half-brother, Prince Mindon, who had encouraged the rebellion, was placed on the throne. Mindon was said to have been a devout Buddhist who abhorred warfare. As such, he readily came to the table to discuss terms of peace with the British.

King Mindon Min's delegation met with the British in March of 1853 and pleaded with them to relinquish the territory of Pegu, but the British, knowing how weak a hand the Burmese had, refused to give up their gains. As peaceful as Mindon Min may have been, he could not agree to these terms, so he cut off communication with the British in May of 1853. But despite this breakdown, an uneasy standoff would lead to a return of fairly cordial relations over the next few years. Unofficial channels through irregular diplomacy were opened, which began to promote a much friendlier dialogue between the two nations.

In the meantime, two distinctly different Burmas were shaping up. There was British Burma, which cobbled together the British holdings of Pegu, Arakan, and Tenasserim, and then there was the traditional Burma, which consisted of the remnants of the old Burmese kingdom overseen by the king, Mindon Min. Consolidating what little territory he had left, Mindon Min instituted a new capital in 1860, making Mandalay the new seat of power.

During this period, King Mindon attempted to reform his government, hoping to make his kingdom robust and dynamic enough to keep the British from absorbing even more territories. However, despite all of his efforts, by 1875, the British had gained even more of his ancestral land. The trouble began when the people of the Karenni States, called Karens, rebelled against the Burmese king and attempted to break away. The Burmese king obviously wasn't just going to allow this insurrection of Karens to take place under his watch, so he tried to rein in the rebellion. King Mindon sent in his forces to take control of the rebellious region, but this put Burmese troops right on the borderlands of British Burma. The Brits made their displeasure known and sent their own forces into the region to aid the Karens.

Initially, the British worked out a deal that would have the Burmese government recognize Karen autonomy, thereby creating another strategic buffer between the British and the Burmese. However, King Mindon died just a few years later, breathing his last in 1878. Thibaw Min, Mindon's son, rose to power. Initially, Thibaw Min seemed like someone who could be controlled by his ministers and who would therefore give more leeway for compromise when it came to the governance of the region. But after his wife, Supayalat, suspected that several ministers were plotting against her husband, she convinced the king to have several of them, as well as many members of his own family, executed. This act shocked the British, and when the court was questioned about it, Thibaw Min's officials simply stated that the king was within his rights to rule his own sovereign realm as he saw fit. Burmese and British relations continued to deteriorate.

While Thibaw Min was giving the British the cold shoulder, he was opening up a new dialogue with the French, who were also making rapid inroads in Southeast Asia. This greatly distressed the British, as they were seeking to keep the French from colliding with their own interests in the region. By this point, the British were seeking a pretext to take action against the Burmese kingdom, and by 1885, they seemed to have found it.

Around this time, a local squabble erupted involving the so-called Bombay Burmah Trading Corporation. This was a British company that had been involved in the extraction of trees from the teak forests of Upper Burma for many years, doing so under a direct agreement with the Burmese kingdom. King Thibaw Min had claimed that the company had illegally taken more trees than was stated in their official contract, and therefore, it had short-changed the Burmese government.

The case went to court in Burma, and the British contractors ended up being fined a lot of money. Predictably, British representatives were upset over this move, and they claimed that the charges were false and that the king's corrupt government was simply trying to extract extra money from the British. The British then ordered the Burmese to appoint a British mediator in order to come to a fair agreement.

However, the Burmese refused to oblige the British, leading the Brits to rather belligerently issue their infamous ultimatum on October 22nd, 1885. This ultimatum demanded that a British representative be installed in Mandalay, and it also insisted that any fines or other legal punishments that had been leveled against the contractors be put on hold until the representative arrived. This wasn't the end of the demands, for the ultimatum contained a clause that didn't seem to have much to do with this local dispute at all. According to the ultimatum, Burma would have to consult with Britain should they wish to conduct business with any foreign country. This was obviously an attempt to curtail Burma's growing relations with the French, and it was a complete affront to Burma's own free will, independence, and sovereignty. The king, of course, knew that if he agreed to this ultimatum, he would become merely a puppet in the hands of the British.

So, predictably enough, he refused to give it another thought. This refusal was all the British needed for their pretext to launch what would become the Third Anglo-Burmese War. It's almost a stretch to call this campaign a war. British troops were sent to Upper Burma on November 14th, and by November 28th, Mandalay was in their hands with very little resistance, and King Thibaw was deposed. This almost unclimactic series of events finally led to the downfall of Burma.

Chapter 7 – Vietnam, Laos, and Cambodia Opened to the World

"Fear keeps us focused on the past or worried about the future. If we can acknowledge our fear, we can realize that right now we are okay. Right now, today, we are still alive, and our bodies are working marvelously. Our eyes can still see the beautiful sky. Our ears can still hear the voices of our loved ones."

-Thich Nhat Hanh

Vietnam, Laos, and Cambodia had spent thousands of years as separate entities until the French came along and decided to cobble them all together in what would become French Indochina in the mid-1800s. As was often the case with the great European powers of the 19th century, it took the flimsiest of pretexts to launch an ambitious spate of colonization to the far-flung corners of the globe. And this is precisely what happened in the lead-up to the French creation of Indochina.

France had been looking for a reason to carve some territory out of Southeast Asia for some time, and when French Christian missionaries were heard to have been mistreated in Vietnam—or as it was called then, *Dai Nam*—it was all the reasoning that Napoleon III needed to send in French troops to pacify the Vietnamese. It could be argued that

Napoleon III was engaging in a bit of "wag the dog" here since embarking on a foreign distraction in Southeast Asia proved to be a great distraction to the political turmoil that was taking place in France.

Napoleon III, who was the nephew of none other than Napoleon Bonaparte himself, had circumvented the French constitution and seized power for himself. He had been democratically elected to serve a term from 1848 to 1852 prior to engaging in a coup d'état, which had him propped up as dictator. Surely not all of the French were happy with these developments, so when Napoleon III had a chance to turn attention abroad, he leaped at the chance.

Although the French punitive expedition was initially meant to teach the Vietnamese a lesson, it became an all-out colonization effort. The French assault began in the southern reaches of Vietnam, where French forces then marched north and took the city of Da Nang in the fall of 1858. This siege included the use of some 14 gunships and nearly 4,000 troops. The Vietnamese fiercely resisted any attempts by the French to move farther north, and after a few months of being repulsed from northward progress, the French decided to head south to attack the southern city of Saigon (modern-day Ho Chi Minh City) instead.

Saigon did not have the defensive networks that the cities of Central and North Vietnam had, so it was relatively easy for the French to take the city. It fell to French forces on February 17th, 1859. But once the French took over Saigon, they met with heavy resistance in the surrounding countryside, making it difficult to move far beyond the city of Saigon itself. The French actually decided to enter into peace talks with the Vietnamese in November of 1859, demanding a treaty in which the Vietnamese would pledge to ensure the safety of the Christian clergy in the future.

However, the Vietnamese leadership refused to enter into any agreements, so the battle raged on. The French, in the meantime, were able to bolster their strength with more reinforcements, and in 1861, they were able to march on several strategic settlements along the

Mekong Delta in southern Vietnam. These territorial gains led to the signing of the Treaty of Saigon on June 5th, 1862. This treaty guaranteed the religious freedom of Christians in the region, and it also opened up the Mekong Delta to French traders.

According to this agreement, the government of Vietnam had to hand over Bien Hoa, Gia Dinh, and Dinh Tuong, as well as the isles of Poulo Condor. The Vietnamese were also stiffed with the bill for the war and were told to fork over a considerable sum of money. By 1864, the territories of Bien Hoa, Gia Dinh, and Dinh Tuong had been made into a colony, which the French called Cochinchina. The French were then able to expand even farther in 1867 when, after another military defeat, the Vietnamese were forced to cede the regions of Ha Tien, Chau Doc, and Vinh Long.

The next step on the path to French Indochina was neighboring Cambodia, which became a French protectorate later that year. The French, in the meantime, had their eyes on using the Mekong as a means of transport to China. But when the Mekong proved too treacherous, they decided to create a path to China by train, constructing a railroad track originating out of Tonkin (a region in northern Vietnam). The region was not exactly friendly to French interests, and after a French official named Francis Garnier was attacked and beheaded by locals in 1873, the French used the incident as justification to enforce their will. After a steady pressure campaign, both Tonkin and the region of Annam were ultimately made into French protectorates.

China couldn't help but notice these troubling developments in its own backyard, and soon, it would be pulled into a conflict with the French. After the French stormed into Hanoi in the spring of 1882, the Chinese sent in an army of their own to confront the French. Initially, the Chinese tried to negotiate with the French, but the French forces by this point were ready to take Vietnamese territory by force.

Unable to reason with the invaders, China began to take up arms against them, and the so-called Sino-French War erupted in 1884 as a result. As the war heated up, the French sent their gunboats as far afield as Taiwan, where they laid waste to Chinese defensive positions. But as successful as the French were on the water, the Chinese made some headway on land when their infantry managed to push the French troops out of Lang Son. The French were not willing to expend their resources in a long, drawn-out war with China, and they were finally convinced to come to the table.

The subsequent peace talks resulted in the Treaty of Tientsin, with both parties placing their signatures on it in June of 1885. As a result of this treaty, the French would be in control of Vietnam. By 1887, the French holdings in Vietnam and Cambodia merged together to form Indochina. The next development was an outbreak of war between France and the Kingdom of Siam (modern-day Thailand) in 1893 when the governor of Indochina sent a French diplomat by the name of Auguste Pavie over to Bangkok to negotiate the placing of Laos under a French protectorate. The Kingdom of Siam refused to consider any such thing, which led the French to engage in "gunboat diplomacy" to produce an outcome that would be favorable to them. With the heavy artillery of the French Navy encircling Bangkok, King Chulalongkorn (also known as King Rama V) of Siam pleaded with the British for help, but the Brits proved to not be of much use. After washing their hands of the whole matter, they basically told King Chulalongkorn to cut a deal with the French. This forced bargain led to the French acquisition of Laos.

King Chulalongkorn is still remembered as a great king among the Thai people, noted for his massive additions to Thailand's infrastructure. This includes modernization efforts to bring electricity and other amenities to the nation. But when it came to French pressuring for Laos, it seemed that the king of Siam was forced to play a losing hand. He knew that his nation would not be able to stand up to the French military on its own, so Chulalongkorn began to seek ways to strengthen the standing of Thailand as an independent nation on the diplomatic front. It was with this purpose in mind that the ambitious Siamese monarch left his homeland for a tour of Europe in 1897. This marked the first official delegation from Thailand, and King Chulalongkorn used all of his diplomatic prowess with the heads of Europe to make sure that his kingdom—or at least what was left of it— would remain free.

In the early 1900s, the borders of French Indochina would go through some slight adjustments, but for the most part, it remained in place. However, this French establishment of a status quo belied the inner turmoil brewing within the borders of French Indochina, as several underground resistance movements were well underway. But it wouldn't be until the strain of World War Two that the French grip on the region would finally be loosened enough for these movements to truly take root.

Chapter 8– Islands of Discovery—The Philippines

"The Philippines is a terrible name, coming from Spain. Philip II was the father of the inquisition, who I believe died of syphilis. It is my great regret that we didn't change the name of our country."

-Imelda Marcos

The Philippines is a dynamic archipelago of around 7,641 islands located in Southeast Asia. These islands make up some 115,831 square miles, with the islands of Mindanao and Luzon making up the vast bulk of the region. Luzon boasts the capital city of Manila, which was the seat of the ancient Kingdom of Tondo, which ruled from 900 CE until the Spanish came along and took over the islands in the 1500s. Prior to the arrival of the Spaniards, the people of the Philippines were heavily influenced by India. After all, it was the Indian subcontinent that helped shape the culture, religion, and even writing of the islands (the Philippines used a form of writing derived from Sanskrit). All of this, of course, was prior to the arrival of Europeans in the region.

Ferdinand Magellan, a Portuguese explorer, who worked for the Spanish Crown, first stumbled upon the Philippines in 1521. In what was indeed a daring voyage for the day, Magellan had sailed from

Europe to the southern tip of South America, rounded the tip, and then continued on in a northwesterly direction across the Pacific Ocean until they ended up off the shores of the Philippines.

There, they made contact with the leader of the islands, Rajah Humabon. The encounter seems to have been a good one, and the rajah even proved to be friendly to Christianity when pressed on the issue. This was important for Ferdinand and his company since they were all fervent Catholics who desired to spread the gospel just as much as they desired to find new lands. After leaving the good graces of the rajah, Magellan and his comrades then made their way to the nearby island of Mactan, but the reception would not be so welcoming there.

In fact, as soon as Magellan's ship landed and he and his crew stepped foot on dry land, they were ambushed by the locals. The attackers seemed to know that Magellan was the leader, and for whatever reason, they directed the bulk of their assault on him. Suddenly, Magellan was having spears thrown at him and scimitar-like blades lunging at his person. Magellan ended up suffering from multiple wounds, and he died right there on the beach. The rest of his shipmates had to quickly dash back to the ship and flee for their lives.

Although the mission would end tragically for Magellan, the rest of the crew would make history nevertheless. After this stop, they would continue west until they were able to circle the tip of South Africa and sail back to Europe, thereby completing the first ever successful global circumnavigation. The Spanish would return to the Philippines decades later in 1565, but this time, it was not as explorers but as conquerors. Led by Miguel López de Legazpi, a group of some 400 Spanish troops took Luzon by force and made Manila the colonial capital of Spain's newest extraterritorial possession.

Manila would become an important center for international trade, as it was now the stopping point for Spanish galleons fresh from Spanish-controlled territories in the Americas. These galleons were typically loaded with silver just mined from Mexico, and with this silver, the Spanish purchased precious goods from China. They essentially worked as an intermediary with Europe, dealing in porcelain, fine spices, and the like.

The Spanish seizure of Manila also had an impact on the Muslim sultanate of Brunei since Manila was considered to be a vassal to the sultan at the time. Brunei had been converted to Islam in the 1400s, some hundred years prior to the arrival of the Catholic Spaniards. After the Spanish converted the Philippines to Christianity in the late 1500s and exerted political control over the region, it wasn't long before an open conflict erupted with the Brunei sultanate. Initially, the Spanish governor of Manila seemed to send the sultan an olive branch, requesting they have friendly relations, but when the governor sought permission to evangelize Brunei with Christian missionaries, the sultan wanted nothing to do with it.

At this time, Spain was an uncompromising religious regime, and ever since the days of the Reconquista when Spanish Christians took back their Iberian Peninsula homeland that had been invaded by the Muslims, the Spanish had been on a never-ending crusade against Islam. When the Spanish Crown decided to declare war on the sultan of Brunei in 1578, this was, in many ways, just the latest battle in this ongoing ideological war.

In Spain's base in Mexico, which was yet another territory that the Spaniards had recently conquered and converted to Christianity, the Spanish had built up a multinational force of Europeans and indigenous Mexicans of various Native American backgrounds, such as Aztecs, Maya, and Incans. This taskforce set sail from western Mexico, traveling across the Pacific Ocean and arriving in the Philippines, where it was reinforced by over a thousand Filipinos.

This fighting force smashed its way into the capital of Brunei—Kota Batu—on April 16th, 1578. The sultan was actually forced to retreat to the higher ground of Jerudong. The Spanish forces were getting ready to chase after him, but they had to call off any further engagements after their camps were rocked by a terrible epidemic of dysentery and cholera.

Weakened from illness, the Spanish retreated back to the Philippines. Relations between Spain and Brunei would eventually normalize, and in 1599, full relations were restored with the understanding that neither side would interfere with the religious affairs of the other. Spanish rule would continue uninterrupted until 1762, which was when the Philippines were briefly taken over by the British.

Spain had been dragged into the so-called Seven Years' War on the side of the French, who were fighting the British. Britain was merciless in its assault on Spanish colonies, assaulting Cuba while simultaneously launching an amphibious invasion of Manila in the Philippines. The British had sent a naval expedition from their colonies in the subcontinent of India, which reached Manila Bay on September 26th, 1762.

This led to the Battle of Manila Bay, in which the Spanish defenders were fairly easily put down by the British invaders. The British agreed to an official withdrawal in 1764, but they would not disperse all of their troops until 1773. Spain remained in control of the Philippines until the territory was lost to the Americans in the Spanish-American War in 1898.

Chapter 9 – The Coming of the Colonists and Capitalists

"I hate imperialism. I detest colonialism. And I fear the consequences of their last bitter struggle for life. We are determined that our nation, and the world as a whole, shall not be the plaything of one small corner of the world."

- Sukarno

The colonization of Southeast Asia followed a fairly standard formula in which European powers would ask a Southeast Asian nation for certain concessions and then use any refusal as a pretext to take them over outright. This occurred in Vietnam when it was demanded upon the Vietnamese government to ensure the protection of Christian missionaries as well as to open up the doors for more widespread trade. When the king of Vietnam refused to appease the French in these demands, Napoleon III decided to launch an invasion in 1858, which would lead to several decades of French consolidation of territory in Southeast Asia.

The same pattern repeated itself in many other locales in the region during this period. Most of the kingdoms of Southeast Asia found themselves at a serious disadvantage when faced with the encroaching

Europeans who were just coming off of the Industrial Revolution, which allowed them to make major strides in the advancement of their armed forces. The disparity between the heavily armed Europeans and the lightly armed Southeast Asians is precisely what led to these instances of so-called gunboat diplomacy. In these instances, steel-hulled freighters suddenly showed up at Southeast Asian ports with artillery fully capable of blasting settlements to smithereens if certain demands were not met.

Indonesia was yet another region of Southeast Asia that faced several waves of colonization, but the first real colonizers of this piece of Southeast Asian real estate actually weren't the Europeans but rather a steady stream of Islamic power brokers who began arriving on the scene sometime in the late 1200s. By the time the Portuguese set their sights on the island of Sumatra in the late 1400s, it was firmly under Muslim control.

The exact process of this Islamization is not exactly clear. This transformation was documented in some local legends, but most modern readers—quite frankly—might have a hard time believing them. An Arab scholar named Ibn Battuta visited the region in 1345, for example, and relayed a rather startling story. In regard to how Islam took hold, he related an account of an Indonesian king called Merah Silau who experienced a miraculous conversion.

According to Ibn Battuta, Merah had a vision of Muhammad, in which the prophet spit in his (Merah's) mouth. Shortly thereafter, Merah was supposedly confounded to find himself speaking strange speech. The legend then goes on to claim that soon after, a merchant craft from the Islamic world popped up, and the visitors were able to inform the befuddled king that the odd words coming out of his mouth were the Islamic confession of faith. This tale would have us believe that an Indonesian king miraculously became a Muslim overnight and that his kingdom followed in his footsteps.

If true, this certainly would be quite unique in the history of Islamic conversions since most other instances of nation states turning to Islam occurred after they were conquered by Muslim armies. The Middle East, all of North Africa, and, for a time, even Spain had become Muslim after military conquests. Upon their military defeat, the citizens were typically given the choice of either becoming Muslims or paying the jizya—a tax non-Muslims had to pay in order to keep their religious freedom intact.

As it pertains to Indonesia, however, there is some evidence that perhaps the assimilation of Islam among the locals was a more gradual process involving the influence of powerful Muslim merchants visiting the region over time. But whatever the case may be, by the time the Portuguese arrived on the scene in May of 1498, Islam was firmly entrenched in the region.

The Portuguese were not exactly the most ardent of missionaries, and most of the time, the trade of expensive spices took precedence over the winning of souls. When the Portuguese erected their first small outposts in and around Indonesia, their main concern was loading up their ships with as many valuable commodities as they could so they could then barter them to merchants in the port cities of Europe. The interesting thing about the Portuguese who took daring trips in the early days of European colonization is that many of them gave up any notion of returning home and instead hung their hat in their outposts in Southeast Asia for good.

In fact, more often than not, Portuguese sailors integrated themselves into the local community as much as they could. They married Southeast Asian women and raised whole families. As daring as many of their exploits were in sailing through uncharted waters, much of the time, they were more likely to be assimilated into Southeast Asia rather than actually colonize the region.

However, all of that would change when Dutch explorers arrived around the year 1596. The Dutch had suffered greatly during their voyage, with many of their number perishing from diseases such as dysentery during the trip. Some of the more abrasive Dutchmen had nearly mutinied and sparked fighting amongst the crew. As such, by the time this discontented lot landed in Indonesia, they were a sorry sight to see, as they were sickly, battered, and bruised (literally) from their own incessant infighting.

Nevertheless, they were received well enough by the locals, and they were given every common courtesy that was given to all foreign traders who arrived in the region. They were also given some assistance by the Portuguese who lived on the islands, as they arranged for the Dutch to be introduced to the local potentate. The Dutch explorers were invited to the king's palace, where they signed a basic treaty that recognized their rights to conduct trade in the region.

However, upon going to the local markets, the Dutch were not happy with what they deemed to be price gouging by local sellers. With such high prices on local spices, they realized that they would not be able to make a decent profit for their efforts. The leader of the Dutch explorers, Cornelis de Houtman, apparently was so incensed that he went to the palace and angrily complained. In the process, he managed to infuriate the king's court and was subsequently ordered off of the island.

The crafty Cornelis agreed to leave, but before he did so, he told his men to cause a ruckus. It's said that these devious Dutchmen started a melee, which left several civilians dead, before hopping on their craft and then turning their artillery on the palace itself. They shelled the king's own court, causing extensive damage before sailing off across the waters. As far as international relations go, this first exposure of the Indonesians to the Dutch was just about as bad as it could have been. There would be time to make amends, and by the early 1600s, more

Dutch ships would reach Southeast Asia and develop much more cordial relations.

Initially, the Dutch outposts that were established didn't have much to do with colonialism as they did sheer, unbridled capitalism. The Dutch knew that if they could get their hands on a ready supply of spices, they would dominate European markets, as just a small amount of precious spice could bring in tremendous profits. In order to make the most of their financial gains, the financial backers of the Dutch expedition created an official commercial enterprise, which they called the Dutch East India Company. This organization would create the first permanent Dutch outpost in Indonesia, in Banten in western Java. Shortly after the installment of the Dutch in Java, the British, who were maritime rivals, tried to dislodge them.

The British would come to haunt Dutch outposts all over the world. After all, it was the British who famously evicted the Dutch from their settlements in Northeastern America, which they called New Amsterdam. After kicking the Dutch out, the victorious British renamed it New York. The British had tried a similar maneuver in the early 1600s when they tried to push the Dutch out of Java. The Dutch, realizing that they were outgunned, sent for reinforcements while a small faction remained besieged in their island fortress. The British soon tired of the expedition and called off the assault. Shortly thereafter, Dutch reinforcements arrived, and the capital of Jakarta was seized and made into the headquarters of the Dutch East Indies.

The Dutch consolidated their power in the region, and by the year 1682, they were influential enough to demand that the local Indonesian leaders of Banten no longer do business with the British. Although this was decades in the making, the Dutch were finally able to deliver their vengeance upon their archrivals by rendering them *persona non grata* as it pertained to Indonesia.

But as influential as the Dutch were at this point, they were still not colonists in the traditional sense. They merely held onto a powerful outpost in Java. However, throughout the 1700s, the Dutch would slowly gain more and more territory in the region. It was as if the Dutch East India Company transformed from a commercial enterprise into something more akin to a colonial territory. In the process, the Dutch monopoly of maritime trade began to decline.

Part of the reason for this decline was simply due to a decrease in the demand for the spices that the East Indies had to offer. The European thirst for items such as cloves and nutmeg had decreased. In addition to this disinterest, British and French colonies were now growing many of these spices on their own, thereby creating a glut in the market, lowering the price of what was previously a precious commodity. The Dutch just weren't making money off spices like they used to. By 1799, due to massive mounting debt, the Dutch East India Company was disbanded, and what could be called a Dutch colony formed in its place. During this time, the Dutch began to turn their attention inward, particularly on the islands of Sumatra and Java, where they began to coerce the locals into growing profitable sugar and rice crops, which could still bring them some profits on the international market. The Dutch administrators profited from this practice, but the locals they induced to labor for them earned very little for their work.

However, it would be wrong to say that the Dutch did nothing to help their colonial subjects, for the people of Indonesia certainly benefited from the Dutch colonial order, as it protected them from the banditry that had been rife in the region in the past. The locals were also given access to quality healthcare, and as a result, they saw an increase in their overall lifespan. The fact that Indonesians were living longer and healthier lives is easily demonstrated by the population growth on the islands while under Dutch rule.

It is said, for example, that in 1800, there were only ten million people who lived on Java. By 1900, that population had tripled to thirty million, which bears testament to the increase in the quality of life that occurred under the Dutch colonial administration. At the dawn of the 20th century, the Dutch decided to be even more humane to their subjects by instituting public welfare initiatives that expanded access to schools and healthcare clinics. This was done in a legislative move they dubbed as their Ethical Policy. Ironically enough, it was the improved education system in Indonesia that taught many for the first time the ideals of democracy, which led to a rethinking of the colonial system that they were under.

The French, in the meantime, had forged their own mighty colony in Southeast Asia, which they referred to as Indochina, of which Vietnam, Cambodia, and Laos were a part. These countries had very little in common with each other besides the fact that they were forced into a union as part of a French colony. Nevertheless, the French were able to profit considerably from their colonial holdings through the development of raw materials, such as rubber and other valuable trade goods. But even so, the administration of their faraway Southeast Asian colony was often a strain on mainland France. The French had to send an endless stream of French bureaucrats just to run the place. The colonial structure also wasn't very good for the locals since it deprived them of the chance to have local representatives stand for them in government, as French colonial officials were sure to take all of these roles for themselves. This meant that local workers had no way to address grievances, for example, when faced with inhumane conditions when working on rubber tree plantations. Although the French introduced capitalism to their colonial society of Southeast Asia, the local populace was more likely to be victimized by this cutthroat form of capitalism than to have any tangible benefit from it.

Things weren't much better in British-controlled Burma either. The British took over Burma in three successive waves, which culminated in the seizure of all Burmese territory at the end of the Third Anglo-

Burmese War. The British then incorporated these new territorial gains with their holdings in neighboring India. The British were brutal at times when rebellions broke out, especially in Lower Burma, where whole villages were sometimes burned down by British troops.

In an effort to divide and conquer the Burmese, the British often helped foster resentment between various ethnic groups. The British showed favoritism to the Karens of eastern Burma, for example, and gave special perks to Indian immigrants. The Burmese were especially resentful of Indians who came and bought lands that had previously belonged to the Burmese. By the turn of the century, the situation was getting especially tense in British Burma, and several anti-Indian rights movements began to break out as the unrest among the Burmese continued to grow.

In the Philippines, a new colonial aspirant had emerged in the form of the United States. The US had wrested the Philippines from its old colonial overseers, the Spanish, after the Spanish-American War of 1898. However, once the US gained the Philippines, they didn't quite know what to do with it. Initially, they had feigned sympathy to Filipino rebels, who had been previously struggling to free themselves from Spain. But just about as soon as the US drove the Spanish out, any pretense of liberation had been dropped. Instead, the US annexed the Philippines as its own territory. The Filipinos, who desired freedom, were not going to take this lying down, and they quickly staged an insurgency against the US occupation. A major battle broke out between the Americans and the insurgents on February 4th, 1899.

This knock-down, drag-out fight would become known as the Battle of Manila, and it was the opening action of the Philippine-American War. This battle erupted after a skirmish broke out on the perimeter of Manila, which the US Army was occupying at the time. And what was a minor incident soon spiraled into an all-out war. Some Filipino insurgents tried to take the initiative by taking control of US artillery, but their advantage wouldn't last for long.

The next day, the US troops rallied and began to seize the surrounding territory around Manila, driving out the rebels. The US control of Manila was secured, but guerilla warfare carried on over the next few years. It was not until the summer of 1902 that American forces could claim to have complete authority over the Philippines, and even then, some sporadic attacks were staged off and on against the occupiers.

Part of the reason why the Filipino insurrection against the United States died down was due to a lack of public support among the majority of Filipinos. The long animosity that had galvanized the Filipinos to revolt against the Spanish was just not there when it came to the Americans. For one, the US ran its colony differently from the European model. The US installed a democratically elected legislature and allowed Filipinos to fill every position with the caveat that the US had to approve all major decisions.

In truth, among the general population of the Philippines, the Americans were considered to be the lesser evil when compared with the Spanish taskmasters who preceded them. Just the fact that the US enabled the separation of church and state was a great improvement on the lives of most Filipinos, who previously had to deal with a domineering Catholic Church that dictated just about every aspect of their lives. The Spanish had given local priests considerable powers that they then imposed upon the laity.

Although the US did nothing to interfere with Catholic worship, leaving Catholic churches to stand where they were, US officials made sure that church and state were separated. Such things were brand new concepts to the Filipinos, and they indeed benefited from them. And as the Filipino people began to experience at least a slight increase in their own personal freedoms, they realized that their yoke was much lighter under the American administration.

But no matter how it was administered, the United States, which was itself a former colony of the British, always seemed rather ill-fit to have an overseas colony. The Philippines was far from the US (although not quite as far as they were from Spain), and most Americans knew next to nothing about Filipino culture.

Then again, the Philippines provided a strategic foothold for US interests in the Pacific when the rising power of Japan made its presence known. Pretty soon, it would be the sudden surge of Japanese imperial might that would come to shake all of these Southeast Asian colonies to their very core.

Chapter 10 – Southeast Asia Consumed by the Co-Prosperity Sphere

"To advocate a New Order was to seek freedom and respect for peoples without prejudice, and to seek a stable basis for the existence of all peoples, equally, and free of threats."

- Tojo Hideki

Japan shocked the world on September 27th, 1940, when it was announced that they had signed on to the so-called Tripartite Pact with Nazi Germany and Fascist Italy. Japan had been a rising power ever since the so-called Meiji restoration began in the 19th century, which helped Japan revitalize its armed forces and industrial base. Rather than falling prey to colonization like so many of its Asian peers, Japan had become a colonial power in its own right.

In 1894, Japan went to war with China and wrested control of Taiwan from the Chinese. In 1904, Japan fought Russia to a standstill, and in 1905, it made Korea a protectorate. This laid the groundwork for Japan to annex the entire Korean Peninsula into its burgeoning empire in 1910. Imperial Japan seemed to have plenty of potential, but other world powers weren't quite sure what the Japanese would do with it.

The fact that Japan would side with the Nazis and Italian Fascists was quite alarming, to say the least, but even a couple of months prior to this bold move, Japanese Foreign Minister Matsuoka Yosuke had made an announcement that should have put the world on notice. He declared Japanese designs for a Greater East Asia Co-Prosperity Sphere.

Even though most wouldn't have had much of a clue as to what such a thing might mean, it would have tremendous implications on Southeast Asia in the years to come. Even Japan's signing of the Tripartite Pact should be seen in this light since as part of the terms of Japan joining forces with the Germans and Italians was for the latter two parties to recognize that East and Southeast Asia would be Japan's sphere of influence.

After the Germans steamrolled through western Europe and defeated France in June of 1940, the Japanese began to consider the ramifications of what might happen to French-controlled territory in Southeast Asia. France's early knockout blow left the fate of the French colonies up in the air. Japan knew that if it did not step in, Germany could seize the colonies for itself. As it were, in the immediate aftermath of France's devastating defeat, a French puppet state was established in southern France around the city of Vichy.

Vichy France, as it was known, would be rendered Nazi allies. And although Vichy France was allowed to keep their extraterritorial possessions, Japan soon made it clear that it expected to be given special perks and privileges since Vichy France's colonies were in their projected sphere of influence. Japan had already sparked another war with China (the first took place in the late 19th century) in 1931 with the seizure of Chinese Manchuria. Then, in 1937, Japan struck China again, this time seizing several major cities along China's eastern coast, including Beijing, Shanghai, and Nanjing.

The seizure of Nanjing (also called Nanking), which has sometimes been referred to as the Rape of Nanjing, was particularly brutal. As the appellation suggests, the taking of the city was followed by wanton rape and pillaging committed by Japanese soldiers. Much of the world turned a blind eye to these atrocities. It wasn't until Japan joined the Axis and began to seize former European possessions in Southeast Asia that the rest of the world really took notice.

It actually took some soul searching among Japanese war planners to decide on acquiring Southeast Asian territory while the war in China continued to rage. Emperor Hirohito of Japan was not pleased with the fact that the war with China had not yet been won while the Japanese military was preparing to open up a new front in Southeast Asia. Hirohito even stated to one of his staff his belief that the Japanese armed forces were merely trying to deflect from their failure to quickly defeat the Chinese by distracting everyone with a new engagement in Southeast Asia. By doing this, the Japanese could then blame the lack of progress against China on the European colonies, which had deprived Japan of the plentiful resources in their own backyard that would have helped them more easily subdue the Chinese.

At any rate, despite his skepticism, the Japanese emperor allowed the war plans to continue as his generals intended. Japan's military leadership was absolutely convinced that the war in China could not continue unless Japan made use of the abundant resources in Southeast Asia to help fuel the fight.

Thus, Prime Minister Konoe Fumimaro of Japan okayed the implementation of the Co-Prosperity Sphere. Initially, it did not necessarily mean outright war but rather a gradual integration of Southeast Asian nations into the sphere. Most important for Japan was for world powers, such as the United States and the Soviet Union, to recognize Japan's dominance in the region. And of these two, it was perhaps the Soviets that Japan was the most worried about.

Japan and Soviet Russia were in close proximity to each other, so it was quite easy for the two to get into territorial disputes. In fact, prior to the Russian Revolution of 1917, when Russia was still run by the tsar, Japan had successfully waged war against the Russians. The newest incarnation of Russian power, the Soviet Union, was not willing to take any chances with Japan in the future, which resulted in a large military buildup between Soviet and Japanese territory. This was a source of considerable tension.

In 1939, a border skirmish erupted in Japanese-controlled Manchuria between Japanese and Russian troops. Despite their previous victories against the Russians, in this unofficial battle, the Japanese did not fare so well. Before the situation escalated into an actual war, both parties were able to come to a diplomatic solution, reaching a new border agreement in the summer of 1940, just prior to Japan joining the Axis. At this point, the last thing Japan wanted was a conflict with Soviet Russia.

This provided Japan with yet another reason to expand into Southeast Asia rather than risk Russian aggression in their northwestern backyard. The Japanese wanted to keep the Russians off their back for the time being. And even when the Germans decided to double-cross Soviet Premier Joseph Stalin and invade Russia, the Japanese, themselves feeling double-crossed, wanted nothing to do with it.

The first implementation of Japan's so-called Co-Prosperity Sphere came after the Nazis defeated France. With the fall of France, the Nazi puppet state of Vichy France was created, and Japan felt that the former French colonial territory in Southeast Asia was ripe for the picking. Since Vichy France was ostensibly an ally of Nazi Germany, Japan couldn't immediately strongarm the colonies away from France outright. Instead, the Japanese sought to pressure and bully the French into meeting as many of their demands as they could. The first of these demands was a request that France allow the Japanese to station troops in North Vietnam in order to aid Japan's continued struggle against the

Chinese. The Japanese insisted that having a foothold in North Vietnam would be essential in their effort to get the upper hand against Chinese forces. The beleaguered French, predictably enough, didn't disagree, and they gave their approval for the Japanese to begin placing troop deployments in North Vietnam. This was initially meant to be just a small troop detachment, but it wasn't long before there were several thousand Japanese soldiers stationed in North Vietnam.

The next demand that the Japanese squeezed out of the French was full control of the port city of Haiphong, citing it as being vital to their war efforts. Soon, Japan was sending troops at will, establishing airbases, and generally making use of whatever resources they could. By the fall of 1940, it was quite clear who was actually in control of French Indochina. Initially, many of the local Vietnamese freedom fighters in the region must have looked upon the Japanese as liberators, but any hopes that the Japanese had their best interests at heart were rather quickly dashed.

Demonstrating their contempt and lack of any real sympathy for the Vietnamese, the Japanese administrators kept much of the French colonial bureaucracy in place. Nothing really changed for the average Vietnamese resident except for the fact that the Japanese had the final say in what the French colonial authorities could do, and at the end of the day, it was the Japanese who were exacting a profit from their labors. Despite any pretense of being liberators, the fact remained that it was much easier for the Japanese to rule through the French than without them.

Another test to Japanese dominion and the status of French Indochina emerged in June of 1940 when Thailand seized upon French weakness and began saber-rattling against the colonists. Even before France was dragged into World War Two, a steady movement had been growing in Thailand to reclaim the lands that France had taken. These sentiments gained real momentum in 1938 when Thai dictator

Field Marshal Plaek Pibulsongkram (better known as Phibun) came to power.

Marshal Phibun, riding on a populist wave, began to speak openly of returning Thailand to its former glory. It was with these intentions in mind that, on June 24th, 1939, Phibun changed the name of his nation from the hated "Siam," which outsiders had essentially given the region, in favor of "Thailand." This name signified that their nation was a home for all Thais, including those currently living under French colonial rule. For an opportunist like Phibun, it must have seemed like the divine hand of fate when German tanks defeated France in 1940. It must have appeared to Phibun that this was just the right time to take on his defeated French nemesis and demand the repatriation of land that France had carved off from Thailand in the past.

Phibun galvanized the Thai armed forces to his cause and launched a war against the French in the region in October of 1940. The French were heavily outnumbered by the Thai troops, and initially, the war went in their favor. By January 6th, 1941, the Thai troops seemed to be close to a major victory in Laos. However, the situation would change rather dramatically only a week later when the beleaguered French cobbled together what remained of their naval craft and launched a sneak attack on January 17th.

The French would turn the tide at the so-called Battle of Ko Chang. This naval battle pitted a French flotilla against a group of Thai craft, and the Thai ships were decimated. This was a devastating blow to the Thai war effort. Although the Japanese were initially content to let the two parties fight it out, after this French victory, they decided to step in and serve as a mediator between the two. Under Japanese "diplomacy," the French were forced to cede the disputed territories to Thailand, and the fighting between the two parties ceased.

The Japanese used their role not as much for peace but rather as a means to further take advantage of the situation. It was from this point forward that Japan would begin to move its own troops into Thailand.

As a result, the Thai state would essentially become an occupied puppet of the Japanese. In fact, the Japanese launched an invasion of Thailand on the very same day that they bombed Hawaii's Pearl Harbor.

Phibun's troops vainly tried to hold the Japanese off, but after one day of fighting, Phibun surrendered to Japanese aggression. Phibun would then decide to collaborate with the Japanese, which led to Phibun openly declaring war on the Allied powers on January 25th, 1942. Thailand, of course, was never considered much of a serious threat in the grand scheme of things, but certain Allied powers, such as the British, in particular, would not forget Phibun's perceived treachery.

Meanwhile, homegrown Vietnamese resistance against the Japanese would begin to take shape under the leadership of the communist idealogue Ho Chi Minh. Since Japan was ramping up its efforts against China and squeezing all manner of resources out of French Indochina, the US Department of State began to take a keen interest in the region. In a bid to slow down the Japanese war machine, the US slapped the Japanese with sanctions, stopping the flow of oil and gas from America to Japan. The British and the Dutch also cut off Japan shortly thereafter.

Japan was dependent on these resources, and without them, it would have to look for more supplies elsewhere. In particular, Japan began to eye British and Dutch holdings in Southeast Asia. However, Japanese war planners were fully aware that any attack on British territory would most likely drag them into a war with the United States. Britain was already fighting off the Germans, and if Japan joined the fray, the United States would surely follow.

At this point, the Japanese figured that war with the US was all but inevitable, so they made the fateful decision to strike out at the Americans first. This preemptive strike came on December 7th, 1941, when the Japanese launched a raid on Pearl Harbor. Similar to the blitzkrieg lightning war that Germany had conducted to quickly overwhelm western Europe, the Japanese hoped to completely cripple the US fleet that was stationed in Pearl Harbor, Hawaii.

Some of the best US battleships, such as the USS *Arizona*, USS *West Virginia*, USS *Oklahoma*, USS *California*, USS *Utah*, USS *Nevada*, and USS *Pennsylvania*, among countless others, were literally blown out of the water. Most were caught completely by surprise, which means they did not even have the chance to take evasive action before their ships were demolished and their crews sent to a watery grave. In all, some 3,500 Americans were killed. With the Americans still digging out the wreckage at Pearl Harbor, the Japanese then unleashed an assault upon British, Dutch, and American holdings in Southeast Asia.

The Japanese seized the Philippines on December 8th, fighting with such ferocity that the unprepared American fleet was forced to evacuate to Java by December 12th, 1941. The Japanese troops that participated in the invasion had been stationed in nearby Formosa, and as soon as they were given the signal, they leaped into action. Incredibly enough, even though the Japanese delivered a blistering defeat to American forces that day, the Americans actually held the numerical advantage. There were indeed more defenders than assailants during the assault on the Philippines, but it is said that many of the colonial troops were inexperienced or irregular units who just did not have the wherewithal to stand up against battle-hardened Japanese troops. In the end, 23,000 American soldiers died or were made prisoners of war, as well as some 100,000 Filipino troops who were also either killed or made prisoners of war.

The Japanese then launched attacks on British-held Malaya, forcing British defenders to retreat to Singapore. After a protracted siege, the Japanese were able to lay claim to Singapore itself on February 15th, 1942. The Japanese war machine then rolled through British Burma, the Dutch East Indies, and other locales, one after the other.

The American defenders who were left behind in the Philippines were forced to surrender to the Japanese on April 9th, 1942. These prisoners of war would come to face some of the worst conditions imaginable. They were routinely beaten, abused, and humiliated, and they were also made to march for long hours with hardly any food or water. One of the most famous of these marches, the so-called Bataan Death March, which had some 80,000 prisoners of war march about 60 miles to their new site of detainment, resulted in several thousand deaths.

With the Japanese controlling both the Dutch East Indies (Indonesia) and the Philippines, the waters around Australia were practically encircled by hostile Japanese troops. Many Australians were concerned that they might be next, but the Japanese would not get that far. That is not to say there were no casualties. The bombing of Darwin was the largest attack mounted by a foreign power on Australia to this day. Japan destroyed several ships while suffering little in return. The attack on Sydney Harbour saw the deaths of twenty-one Allied soldiers. However, in the grand scheme of World War Two, Australia's casualties were more minor. The gains made in late 1941 and in the first half of 1942 would mark the highpoint of Japan's aggression, as its power would only dwindle from this point forward.

After Japan's disastrous defeat at the hands of the United States at the Battle of Midway Island in June of 1942, the Americans began to slowly but surely push the Japanese back. Midway was an all-around disaster for the Japanese, which saw four of their aircraft carriers destroyed. This fact alone put a significant dent in Japan's ability to wage war. After all, it was their aircraft carriers that had enabled the Japanese bombers and fighters to get within range of Pearl Harbor in December of 1941. Without suitable aircraft carriers, a wrench was thrown into Japan's ability to launch long-range attacks across the Pacific.

The Battle of Midway was followed by another important US victory in the Solomon Islands when the US took on the Japanese at Guadalcanal. The Solomon Islands, which had previously been a British possession before the Japanese took them over, was important to the Japanese because they were a key component of their overstretched supply lines. The Japanese also wished to use the Solomon Islands as a launchpad for further attacks across the Pacific.

However, these plans were foiled when the US launched an invasion of the islands, one that was determined to drive the Japanese out. American Marines fought bloody battles with the Japanese for every inch of land they could get a hold of. And while the Marines duked it out with the Japanese on land, US naval forces took on the Japanese navy in the surrounding waters.

The siege would last until February of 1943 when the last Japanese defenders were finally forced to abandon the islands. Interestingly, as Japanese leaders began to sense that the war was not turning in their favor, more consideration was given to additional autonomy to the Southeast Asian nations that were under their dominion. On January 28th, 1943, the recently elected prime minister, Tojo Hideki (commonly referred to as Hideki Tojo in the Western style, where one's surname appears after their given name), began to openly speak of granting some semblance of independence to both Burma and the Philippines.

It seems that, once again, the Japanese hoped that by presenting themselves as liberators, they could gain the active support of Southeast Asians. These words were followed up with action when Burma and the Philippines were both granted a form of independence on August 1st and October 14th, respectively.

Despite the lip service, Tojo Hideki himself never really believed that the nations of Southeast Asia merited independence. In fact, just a few days prior to Burmese independence, Prime Minister Tojo stated to his colleagues, "Burma is more a newborn than a child," insinuating in his own patronizing way that Japan would have to be the guiding hand of the infantile Burmese. Tojo then further assured his colleagues of Burma's ultimate submission to Japan when he stated, "as long as we have our military power, we know we have Burma by the throat."

The most elaborate bit of pseudo-nation building that the Japanese engaged in was when, on October 21st, 1943, they installed an Indian nationalist named Subhas Chandra Bose in Singapore in what was termed the Provisional Government of Free India. Since Singapore is fairly far removed from India, this was obviously a government in exile, which the Japanese hoped would inspire more independence-minded Indians to support their efforts. It was hoped that Indian nationalists on the subcontinent would look upon the Indian-run government in Singapore with pride and inspire them to turn against their British colonial taskmasters in India proper. The Japanese especially hoped that the sight of an armed and independent Indian army in Southeast Asia would inspire all Indians in the region to join their cause. And before the war was out, the Japanese would indeed have Subhas Chandra Bose's forces march on mainland India in a desperate attempt to dislodge the British hold on the region.

But no matter how much Japan claimed that these various regimes were independent, they were really only independent so long as they followed the wishes of Japan. Nevertheless, on November 5th, 1943, the Japanese high command convened the so-called Greater East Asia Conference, which would attempt to present all of Japan's puppet rulers as equals. This was where the future plans for the Co-Prosperity Sphere were hammered out. Here, Japan's efforts were presented as a collective struggle that involved all of Southeast Asia against Western imperialism.

By 1944, however, it was clear to all that the war was beginning to go very badly for the Japanese, and as the Japanese dug in for a tough fight, promises for true autonomy rang hollow. Japan was now on the defensive against the Allies, and it had lost much of any real support from Southeast Asian nations, such as the Philippines and Burma, the latter of which had Allies landing on its soil in March of 1944.

The Japanese, while being bounced out of Burma, actually caught the Allies off guard by driving westward and invading British India. A force of some 85,000 Japanese soldiers, coupled with additional support from Subhas Chandra Bose's Indian National Army, attempted to assault British positions while simultaneously stirring up popular resentment among the locals. It was hoped that a homegrown resistance to British rule would emerge and that, in the chaos, the British would be defeated. It was also an objective of the Japanese to tie down the British in India so that they would not be able to fight in Burma.

The joint Japanese/Indian forces seized the border town of Imphal on March 29th, 1944, taking the British by complete surprise. The Japanese were then able to shut down the Imphal-Kohima road without much resistance. Emboldened, they then took over the nearby town of Kohima on April 6th. However, the British were not going to take this lying down, and finally, a British/Indian force was assembled to take on the Japanese. This group cut through the blockage of the Imphal-Kohima road, and once a relief force arrived on the scene, the true battle began. The invaders held on for a while, but they ended up retreating completely that July. Driven back to Burma, the Japanese realized they only had a mere toehold left, which was centered around the Irrawaddy River. The Japanese would be kicked out of Burma for good by 1945.

In the meantime, in nearby Vietnam, the Vietnamese resistance to the Japanese was only increasing. The communist-backed rebel forces, known as the Viet Minh, were particularly effective when it came to launching guerilla-styled attacks on the occupying Japanese troops. Nevertheless, by March of 1945, the Japanese had tightened their grip by stripping all French colonies of power so that the Japanese could rule directly over the Vietnamese people. It would be short-lived since the Japanese were inching closer and closer to their ultimate defeat in the Second World War. And as Japan teetered on the very brink of collapse, the Viet Minh actually managed to wrest their own piece of territory from the Japanese in northeastern Vietnam.

This piece of high ground would remain important to the Viet Minh as the group continued its struggle to create an autonomous communist enclave in the decades to come. As Japan neared its inevitable defeat, the Viet Minh grew bolder, and by August, the rebels had actually managed to take both Hanoi and Saigon. Then, on September 2nd, 1945, the Vietnamese rebel leader Ho Chi Minh boldly announced that his Viet Minh had established the first Democratic Republic of Vietnam.

Interestingly enough, this was declared on the very same day that Japan officially surrendered to the Allied forces. However, the Allies didn't take this homegrown declaration of independence very seriously. And, in reality, Ho Chi Minh only controlled a portion of the north, while the French, aided by the British, were attempting to restore the colonial rule in the south. This wasn't an easy task, though, since the communist Viet Minh were roaming the countryside, spreading disorder as much as they could. Things were so bad, in fact, that the British and French actually recruited the recently defeated Japanese to help them fight off the Viet Minh! The Japanese themselves were being consistently assaulted by Vietnamese guerilla fighters, which left them unable to even evacuate themselves from the region until the violence subsided.

As such, the Brits had the French declare martial law until a joint force of French, British, and Japanese troops attempted to put down the ferocious Viet Minh fighters. This feat was finally achieved on September 23rd, 1945. With some semblance of peace restored, the former French colonial infrastructure was put back into place.

Much the same could be said for many other parts of Southeast Asia that the Japanese had withdrawn from. But despite the false promises of the Co-Prosperity Sphere, the nations of Southeast Asia were not going to be satisfied until their true freedom was legitimately realized.

Chapter 11 – Southeast Asia and the Sweet Taste of Freedom

"I did not join the resistance movement to kill people, to kill the nation. Look at me now. Am I a savage person? My conscience is clear."

-Pol Pot

Since much of Southeast Asia had become colonized, the march to freedom was not going to be an easy one. It took local struggles against colonial overlords, two world wars, and further such struggles to achieve something akin to independence, which would then be followed by an attempt to forge statehood from scratch. In much of Southeast Asia, these were the things required in order for any true freedom to take place.

Of all the former colonies to achieve statehood, it was perhaps the Philippines whose road was the easiest. Despite the horrors inflicted upon them by the Japanese, the Japanese occupiers had put a bureaucracy in place of local Philippine leadership, which would serve as the framework for an independent nation state. The Philippines also benefited from the fact that the United States, unlike the British and French, was not absolutely hellbent on keeping the Philippines as a territory. In fact, even before the Japanese occupation, the US had entered into an agreement with the Philippines that aimed to pave the way for a gradual independence by 1946. The plan called for the Philippines to remain under a commonwealth status until full independence could be achieved. The US had even overseen the election of the first president, Manuel Quezon, in 1935. Once the Japanese were kicked out, plans for independence were once again put into place, and the first legitimate independent Philippine state came into being on July 4th, 1946. Although Manuel Quezon had perished from tuberculosis in 1944 while in exile in the United States, a new Filipino president was readily elected in his place.

The British in Burma, on the other hand, had a much more difficult time letting go of their overseas possession. There was a lot of baggage and unfinished business let over after the war, and initially, the British wanted to try those Burmese who had collaborated with the Japanese. Among them was the popular Burmese leader Aung San.

The Burmese revolutionary Aung San had first come to prominence as a student rabble rouser who organized protests against British rule in the 1930s. Aung San eventually went from being a student organizer to leading a revolutionary group, which called itself Thakin. As British authorities began to crack down on the movement, Aung San relocated to Japan in 1940. This, of course, was right on the eve of the eventual Japanese invasion of Burma, an invasion that Aung San had a front seat to, arriving back in Burma in prominence in Burma while riding on the coattails of the Japanese.

Having said that, there was certainly more than enough skeletons in Aung San's closet to merit a closer look by the British, but since Aung San was so popular with the Burmese people, it was quickly realized that such a thing would only make an already chaotic situation even worse. Aung Sang headed the most powerful political party at the time, which was clamoring for independence. This party was the so-called Anti-Fascist People's Freedom League.

With this powerful political backing, Aung San demanded nothing short of complete and full independence from Britain. The British, however, began to stall for time and instead presented a much more gradual process that included a lengthy transition before finally granting Burma its autonomy. This did not at all sit well with the Burmese, and in the fall of 1946, they let the British know by staging massive protests that included a national strike of Burmese police and other low-level bureaucrats. Britain could not ignore this unrest, and by early 1947, British officials were pressured to come to the table.

In January of that year, Aung San himself made his way to London to discuss terms of a final separation of Burma from Britain. It was agreed that a general election would be held that April. Aung San was officially elected by a majority of the Burmese people, although many Karens (an ethnic group in Burma) decided to sit the election out due to lingering feelings of disenfranchisement and frustration with the process. Some believed that by boycotting the proceedings they could convince the incoming administration to approve Karen independence from Burma. At any rate, Aung San would not have long to enjoy his victory, as he was assassinated on July 19th, 1947. The British weren't the ones behind this hit as one might initially expect; it was actually a rival Burmese political party that carried out the hit.

Nevertheless, even though the newly elected prime minister was dead, a new constitution for a free and independent Burma was forged on September 24th, 1947. Aung San's successor, U Nu (also known as Thakin Nu), presided over the British signing of the treaty, which formally acknowledged the new Republic of the Union of Burma on October 17th, 1947. This treaty was officially ratified by the British Parliament on January 4th, 1948, declaring to the world that Burma was indeed a free and independent nation.

But although it was declared free from Britain, Burma would face several decades of tumult and inner turmoil. There would be waves of protest against corruption and multiple outright coups. In the quest to reform the Burmese government, it would be none other than the daughter of the assassinated Aung San, Aung San Suu Kyi, who would rise to prominence as a champion of human rights in Burma. For her efforts, Aung San Suu Kyi was persecuted by the Burmese government and placed under house arrest in 1991. She was finally released in 1995.

Aung San Suu Kyi continued to fight for the rights of the average Burmese citizen, and as a result, she once again ended up in prison in 2000. She was released in 2002, but she was very nearly assassinated in 2003. Nevertheless, in 2010, riding on a tide of popular sentiment, she was elected as state counsellor, which is essentially the Burmese equivalent of a prime minister. Aung San Suu Kyi is well known for her activism, and she is a Nobel Peace Prize winner for her efforts.

However, in recent years, her legacy has been marred by the alleged genocide of Burma's Rohingya ethnic group. It has been claimed that the Burmese military has carried out a systematic genocide of the primarily Muslim Rohingyas and that Aung San Suu Kyi has tried to cover it up. Aung San Suu Kyi actually made an appearance before the International Court of Justice (ICJ) over this issue in 2019, and she not only refused to acknowledge that any genocide ever occurred, but she also defended the actions of the Burmese military. Many around the world who knew her as a human rights activist were quite shocked at this turn of events.

Whatever the case may be, her strong defense of the military certainly didn't do her any favors, and on February 1ˢᵗ, 2021, she was ousted from power in a military coup. Amid claims of widespread irregularities, the results of the previous November election had been thrown out, and Aung San Suu Kyi was forcibly removed from power and placed under arrest. As of publication, both the fate of Aung San Suu Kyi and Burma (Myanmar) remain uncertain.

But as chaotic as the independence of Burma was, it wasn't anywhere near as rough as the Indonesian struggle to free itself from Dutch domination. The Indonesians had declared their independence right at the end of World War Two when the Indonesian revolutionary Mohammad Hatta declared the country's independence on August 17th, 1945. The Dutch, who wished to reestablish themselves as colonial overlords, did not take kindly to this, and it would mark the beginning of a bitter four-year struggle over the fate of Indonesia.

For the average Indonesian, this would become a struggle against each other just as much as it was against the Dutch. The thing that made the Indonesian National Revolution particularly ugly was the fact that hardline revolutionaries came to see prominent Indonesians who had prospered under Dutch rule as enemies to their cause. As a result, it has been claimed that more Indonesians perished from fighting each other during the course of their revolutionary struggle than died at the hands of the Dutch. At any rate, it was only after a major upheaval that the Dutch finally recognized Indonesia as an independent state in December of 1949.

However, even the struggle of the Indonesians pales in comparison to the long, drawn-out saga of the Vietnamese. At the end of World War Two, the Vietnamese guerilla fighters, the Viet Minh, declared independence, much like the Indonesian revolutionaries had. But this declaration was not at all welcomed by the French. With the help of the British, the French reestablished themselves in southern Vietnam while the communist-aligned Viet Minh still had control of the north.

In the spring of 1946, the French came to acknowledge the Democratic Republic of Vietnam (DRV) in the north but insisted that a referendum be held to determine the fate of South Vietnam. Initially, Ho Chi Minh agreed, but the talks broke down, and all-out fighting between the French-controlled south and the communist north erupted anew. The French, in the meantime, tried to put a Vietnamese façade on their presence in South Vietnam by installing Bao Dai, a descendant of the Vietnamese imperial line, as the head of state. In reality, Bao Dai was just a puppet for the French.

In early 1950, the Soviet Union and communist China (Chinese communists took over China in 1949) officially acknowledged the DRV. Since the Cold War between the United States and the Soviet Union was already in full swing, the US was none too pleased with these developments. The United States desired to contain communism, and as the war in Korea was about to prove, the nation was willing to spend much blood and money in order to do so.

Although US troops were not yet in Vietnam by the early 1950s, the US was sending millions of dollars in aid to help prop up the French-backed South Vietnamese. Meanwhile, the North Vietnamese were ramping up their efforts against the South Vietnamese. The North Vietnamese aggression ultimately culminated in the so-called Battle of Dien Bien Phu in the spring of 1954. In a serious of ferocious assaults, the Viet Minh brought the French close to total defeat.

At this point, the French turned to the Americans for help. US President Dwight D. Eisenhower initially intimated that perhaps the United States could conduct some limited bombing campaigns against the North Vietnamese. However, when the notion was brought before the US Congress, it was thoroughly rejected. Eisenhower was not willing to push the issue after that, and the French realized that US military support would not be available any time soon.

As a result of US unwillingness to engage in war, the French were forced to negotiate with the North Vietnamese. This led to a deal in which Vietnam would be officially partitioned into two countries—a communist regime in the north and a French-backed regime in the south. From here on out, the French would no longer have a military presence in South Vietnam, but the United States began to become more and more involved with military aid to the South Vietnamese in a desperate bid to fortify South Vietnam against the communists.

The South Vietnamese Prime Minister Ngo Dinh Diem also received full political support of US officials, even though Diem was increasingly unpopular with the South Vietnamese themselves. Diem was a strident anti-communist, and he systematically cracked down on subversive groups in South Vietnam. However, the more Diem cracked down on them, the more they continued to pop up. Soon, South Vietnam had to deal with the so-called Viet Cong, a communist group backed by the North Vietnamese. In fact, the North Vietnamese had created a vast supply line that ran through neighboring Laos and Cambodia to aid South Vietnamese guerilla fighters. This supply line, which was called the Ho Chi Minh Trail, would become a major thorn in Diem's side. The conflict entered a new phase in November of 1963 when Diem was assassinated. He was then succeeded by a South Vietnamese general named Duong Van Minh, and from here on out, the situation in Vietnam would only get worse.

In 1964, the USS *Maddox* was torpedoed by the North Vietnamese in the Gulf of Tonkin. This led to the so-called Gulf of Tonkin Resolution, which gave US President Lyndon B. Johnson the go-ahead to take military action against the North Vietnamese. This came in the form of a massive bombing campaign conducted against the North in February of 1965 called Operation Rolling Thunder. President Johnson then upped the ante even more by deploying over 180,000 US troops to the region less than a month later.

By 1966, the number of American troops in Vietnam would swell to over 400,000. But no matter how many troops or bombs the Americans threw at the communist Vietnamese, they absolutely refused to give up. Not only that, they only seemed to grow more relentless. After a shocking assault on a US Marine garrison in the South Vietnamese city of Khe Sanh in 1968, the US realized it was stuck in an intractable quagmire. The American defenders of Khe Sanh were able to repel the Viet Minh attackers, but they lost 250 American soldiers in this one battle alone. And even after achieving this hard-won victory, it was clear that it didn't amount to much since the Viet Minh could regroup and attack them all over again.

The real shock would come in the 1968 Tet Offensive when the Viet Minh launched a coordinated massive assault on South Vietnam, attacking over 100 different targets all at once. During the onslaught, even the US Embassy was penetrated, although the invaders were repulsed; however, it came with a great cost of life. By now, the war was incredibly unpopular among the American public, with frequent protests against it staged in cities throughout the United States. Faced with such an unpopular war, President Johnson chose not to run for reelection. Richard Nixon ultimately became the next US president, and he pledged to bring US troops home.

Nixon's strategy to do this was to launch a massive effort to train and mobilize South Vietnamese troops so that they could take up the bulk of the fighting and allow the US soldiers to withdraw slowly. However, along with withdrawing troops, Nixon also broadened the scope of the fighting by directing units to take on the North Vietnamese supply lines that ran through nearby Laos and Cambodia. Nixon began a bombing campaign within the borders of these two nations, which was widely considered illegal at the time. None of these efforts seemed to have much of an impact on the ability of the North Vietnamese to wage war, though, as was proven in the massive Easter Offensive launched by the Viet Minh in 1972.

Even though Nixon was unable to find a military solution to Vietnam, he didn't cease to look for political solutions. He thought he found one when he opened the door to diplomatic relations with China. The fact that Nixon normalized relations with China was a big deal since no previous US president had even bothered to recognize the legitimacy of the Chinese government after China's communist revolution of 1949. However, Nixon and Chairman Mao Zedong found some common ground, and Nixon was able to use China to gain leverage with Vietnam. By using China to pressure the North Vietnamese, the Viet Minh were persuaded to come to the table to negotiate a potential peace deal.

Unfortunately, all of this was derailed in 1973 when Nixon faced his own political pressure from home in the form of the so-called Watergate scandal. Nixon had been implicated in a bungled break-in of the Democratic National Committee's headquarters during the previous year's election. Nixon was ultimately forced to resign, and in the midst of this turmoil, negotiations with the North Vietnamese fell through. In the end, the remaining US troops were forced to withdraw in 1975, and North Vietnam would take over South Vietnam, uniting the country under one government.

Ironically enough, after all of the bloodshed over whether or not Vietnam should become a communist state, Vietnam would drop much of its hardline Marxist policies in subsequent years and embrace many capitalist ideals simply because they made the nation more prosperous in the long run. After a terrible recession in the late 1970s, Vietnam opened up to private enterprises by the 1980s. Farmers, for example, were permitted to sell surplus produce in order to make a profit. Such measures improved the economy, and Vietnam has continued to embrace many aspects of free-market capitalism to this day. In fact, Vietnam is now a trading partner with the United States and even its old nemesis, France. Was all of that fighting in Southeast Asia for nothing? Perhaps looking back, one could say so, but, of course, as they say, hindsight is always 20/20.

But as rough of a transition Vietnam had, in many ways, neighboring Cambodia had an even worse time emerging from colonialism. The French agreed to grant the Cambodians more say in their government after the war, with reforms being enacted in January of 1946. The French also agreed to get rid of some of the old colonial formalities, such as stuffy titles for colonial officials, and they pledged to establish a locally elected legislature under a constitutional monarchy, which would be headed by the Cambodian royal family. At the time, the royal family was headed by King Norodom Sihanouk.

Even though some local affairs were given over to the Cambodians, matters of major importance, such as international relations, military defense, and even internal policing, would all still be left up to the French. All the same, it was the most freedom the French had ever given the Cambodians, and many were eager to see it through.

Cambodia's first set of elections were carried out that spring. The two main parties were the Liberals and the Democrats. From an American perspective, the names of these two parties might be confusing on the surface, but their names don't correlate to American politics. The so-called Liberals are actually the conservative wing of Cambodia, whereas the Democrats are the liberal wing.

Now that this little explanation is out of the way, here's how the first election and the next few elections shaped up. In the first few Cambodian elections, the Democrats won the majority of seats. In fact, in 1946, the Democrats won fifty seats, while the Liberals only won fourteen seats. This was a source of great frustration for both the king and the French-backed Cambodian elites who backed the conservative Liberals in their bid for office.

Things turned violent in January of 1950 when a political activist tossed a live grenade into the Democrats' headquarters in the city of Phnom Penh. This assault killed a major leader of the party, a man named Ieu Koeus. This attack stoked the anger of many in the public, and when the economy began to tank later that year, massive discontent began to erupt in the streets. It was in this volatile atmosphere that another election was held in the fall of 1951.

During this election, the Democrats won a supermajority of fifty-four seats, while the Liberals gained a measly eighteen. The French and the Cambodian elites who had dished out a lot of money to help the Liberals were not happy. In fact, they had reached a breaking point, and a coup was staged in June of 1952 to remove the democratically elected prime minister, Huy Kanthoul.

The French officially left Cambodia in 1953, and King Sihanouk ruled more or less by direct decree over the next several years. There would still be the charade of elections, but now, only the candidates backed by the king would prosper. Although he was essentially a dictator, King Sihanouk had some admirable qualities as a leader. He had a good ear to the ground and understood what both commoners and elitists alike expected of him. He also knew what the wider world expected of him. He knew, for example, that anything to do with communists would make him a pariah to the West. As such, King Sihanouk made sure to distance himself from the communist guerillas fighting in North Vietnam as much as he possibly could while not provoking the communists in the process. And in many ways, the fact that he kept Cambodia out of the Vietnam War for so long was to his credit. He masterfully threaded the needle when it came to staying on the good side of both the Americans and the North Vietnamese. He knew, for example, that the North Vietnamese would not tolerate Cambodia allowing the US to station troops on its soil, so when the US floated the notion, he stood firm behind his convictions.

However, both North Vietnam and the United States would later find ways to circumvent the sovereignty of Cambodia. Vietnamese communists often made use of the Cambodian borderlands, and the US eventually conducted bombing runs across Cambodia's border. Nevertheless, Sihanouk largely stood by his principles of neutrality.

By 1970, however, the winds were once again changing, and in March of that year, Sihanouk, who was no longer the king but rather the head of state, was removed from power. There had been several rounds of riotous protests in the preceding months over North Vietnamese communists who were active in Cambodia. Sihanouk was overseas at the time, visiting several nations, including China, the Soviet Union, and some European countries. While Sihanouk's back was turned, his own prime minister, Lon Nol, plotted against him, declared martial law, and forced Sihanouk out. The new government, borrowing from the greatness of Cambodia's previous Khmer Empire, would be called the Khmer Republic. And it was in this tumultuous backdrop that a young Cambodian communist by the name of Saloth Sar, better known by the name Pol Pot, came to prominence. The communists that Pol Pot led would also become known by their own infamous moniker of the Khmer Rouge. The term "Khmer" is in reference to the Cambodian language and ethnic identity, whereas "Rouge" is the French word for red. Communists have been widely referred to as "reds," so essentially, the name was an epithet to refer to communist Cambodians. It was meant as an insult, but the Khmer Rouge would come to embrace the title.

Soon after the Khmer Republic was declared, Cambodia descended into a civil war, with the communist forces of the Khmer Rouge backed by North Vietnam as they fought against the Cambodian government. This was a real slugfest, and even when President Richard Nixon renewed US bombing campaigns of communist targets in Cambodia, the Khmer Republic was still unable to gain the upper hand. Pol Pot's Khmer Rouge was ultimately successful, and Pol Pot and his so-called Democratic Kampuchea would come to power in 1975—the same year that US troops were practically being chased out of neighboring Vietnam.

Pol Pot, in the meantime, would set up a brutal regime that would leave between 1.5 to 2 million Cambodian citizens dead by the time that its brutality had run its course. The Khmer Rouge was so brutal that they even angered their former communist backers, the Vietnamese. After several border skirmishes, Vietnam invaded Cambodia outright in 1978. Conditions in Cambodia had grown even worse, and with the threat of a Vietnamese invasion, the oppression of Cambodians reached horrific new lows.

Ethnic minorities, such as the Cham and especially those who happened to be of Vietnamese background, were routinely slaughtered. It got so bad that, at one point, it has been said that even conversing in another tongue could get one killed. The Khmer Rouge finally came to an end when the Vietnamese forces forcibly dismantled the regime on January 10th, 1979.

Now under the full weight of outside oppression, Cambodia would not regain its independence until 1989, which was when the last Vietnamese troops finally withdrew. Pol Pot died in 1998 while under house arrest. He was seventy years old, and he apparently died of natural causes, although some believe he committed suicide. To this day, there is tremendous outrage among those who feel that Pol Pot never really answered for his many crimes.

Cambodia would begin to really get its act together by the early 2000s. In 2003, the country was deemed to be prosperous enough to be admitted to the Association of Southeast Asian Nations (ASEAN). Cambodia's ultimate liberation was certainly a long time coming, but just as all of the other Southeast Asian nations that had been freed from the grip of colonialism, the taste of freedom was still just as sweet as ever. However, as in some other Southeast Asian countries, Cambodia faces a crisis when it comes to the government, as the country has been run by one party since 2018, despite labeling itself as a multi-party democracy. Thailand is another country that has faced difficulties in regards to the government, for it has bounced back and forth through military regimes and constitutional monarchies. Since 1932, Thailand has undergone seventeen different constitutions. It is hard to know what the future will hold for countries like Cambodia and Thailand, but considering everything they have gone through and how far they have come, there is hope they will establish governments that promote equality and a strong economy.

Conclusion: Where Legend Meets Reality

Southeast Asia is a land of many legends. All one has to do is think of the spectacular grandeur of Angkor Wat, and this much is made clear. The nations of Southeast Asia have histories that reach back thousands of years, and many countless civilizations have risen and fell during the many varied epochs of Southeast Asian dynasties. These regimes navigated through all manner of political intrigue and engaged in battle after battle with opposing forces.

For example, the Kingdom of Vietnam was shaped by the dueling pressures of China to its north and the Champa regime to its south. It was in the midst of this pressure cooker that the Vietnamese learned to be absolute experts at guerilla warfare. Indonesia, on the other hand, with its prime location between the shipping routes of both China and India, became the ultimate weigh station for trade goods, as well as for religion and culture. Throughout history, the majority of the Indonesian population has been Hindu, Buddhist, and Muslim. It is due to this plurality of beliefs that Indonesia today prides itself as a religiously tolerant society. Indonesia, of course, also benefits from its history in the spice trade, and today, it leads the world in many forms of commerce. In fact, Indonesia boasts one of the biggest and most robust economies in all of Southeast Asia.

However, all of these civilizations are dynamic locales that certainly live up to the hype. Tourism is a big business in Southeast Asia because there is simply always something new to explore. Walking through old Hindu temples or retracing the steps of past adventurers such as Marco Polo, Ibn Battuta, or Ferdinand Magellan, you can sense some of the wonder that the Dutch East India Company must have known. After all, Southeast Asia is no ordinary place. It's not just a collection of peninsulas, tropical coasts, and islands. It's also the land of Brahma, Buddha, Islam, and Catholicism. Southeast Asia is a realm of pure wonder—that neverland where the once imagined is suddenly possible.

Southeast Asia was the fabled spice lands that brought sailors far and wide, and it was the rubber-rich trees that drew in both the French and the likes of Imperial Japan. Southeast Asia is indeed plentiful in resources. But the land of Southeast Asia is not only where the rubber meets the road—Southeast Asia is also where the legend meets reality.

Here's another book by Captivating History that you might like

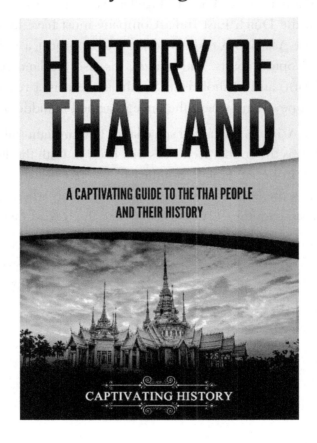

Free Bonus from Captivating History
(Available for a Limited time)

Hi History Lovers!

Now you have a chance to join our exclusive history list so you can get your first history ebook for free as well as discounts and a potential to get more history books for free! Simply visit the link below to join.

Captivatinghistory.com/ebook

Also, make sure to follow us on Facebook, Twitter and Youtube by searching for Captivating History.

Appendix A: Further Reading and Reference

Hall, D. G. E. *Burma*. 1950.

Hannigan, Tim. *A Brief History of Indonesia*. 2015.

Lockhard, Craig. *Southeast Asian World History*. 2009.

Myint-U, Thant. *The Making of Modern Burma*. 2001.

Reid, Anthony. *Charting the Shape of Early Modern Southeast Asia*. 1999.

Stuart-Fox, Martin. *A Short History of China and Southeast Asia: Tribute, Trade, and Influence*. 2014.

Tully, John. *A Short History of Cambodia: From Empire to Survival*. 2005.

Yellen, Jeremy A. *The Greater East Asia Co-Prosperity Sphere*. 2019.

Made in United States
North Haven, CT
29 December 2023

46803192R00059